DUBLIN
1911

Toque hat made of lime-green glossy straw
with ostrich feathers. Fashionable life revolved
around Dublin Castle, and hats were *de
rigueur* with almost 600 milliners in Dublin.

DUBLIN
1911

Edited by

CATRIONA CROWE

with contributions from Paul Rouse, Mark Duncan
and William Murphy

Researcher: Rosie Duffy

RIA

Dublin 1911

First published 2011
by Prism
Prism is an imprint of the
Royal Irish Academy.
19 Dawson Street
Dublin 2

www.ria.ie

Prism aims to disseminate scholarship to a general readership.

ISBN 978-1-904890-79-9

FRONT COVER: Group of children at the beach, paddling in shallow water (1890–1910). Courtesy of the National Library of Ireland (ref: CLAR 29).
FRONT FLAP: Chromolithograph from the Paris fashion house of Atelier Bachwitz. Youthful black British straw hat. Brim turned up all round and faced with a collar shaped flounce of cream lace. The latter is finished off with a smart bow of black ribbon on either side.
BACK COVER: Advertisement: 'Fry's Pure Cocoa'. *Irish Society and Social Review* XXIV (1249) (23 December 1911). Courtesy of the National Library of Ireland (ref: IR 05 i 33, p. 4194).
Advertisement: 'About 250 bakers wanted at once in Dublin'. *Irish Independent*, 4 October 1911, 4.
Advertisement: '"So you are a cyclist?" (J.J. Kelly)'. *Irish Society and Social Review* XXIV (1216) (6 May 1911). Courtesy of the National Library of Ireland (ref: IR 05 i 33, p. 8622).
Advertisement: 'Schreier Ladies' Tailor and Habit Makers'. *Irish Society and Social Review* XXIV (1248) (16 December 1911). Courtesy of the National Library of Ireland (ref: IR 05 i 33, p. 4157).
Advertisement: 'Cole, 18 Lower Sackville Street, Dublin'. *Irish Independent*, 3 April 1911, 1.
BACK FLAP: Advertisement: 'Smith and Pearson Ltd.' *Irish Independent*, 6 July 1911, 1.

British Library Cataloguing in Publication Data. A CIP catalogue record for this book is available from the British Library.

An Roinn
Ealaíon, Oidhreachta agus Gaeltachta
Department of
Arts, Heritage and the Gaeltacht

This publication has received support from the National Archives of Ireland and the Department of Arts, Heritage and the Gaeltacht.

Design: Fidelma Slattery

Printed in Northern Ireland by Nicholson & Bass

10 9 8 7 6 5 4 3 2 1

CONTENTS

THE PASSING OF THE BARBER PERHAPS

It has been seriously suggested that the Coronation Year should be celebrated by the male citizens of the Empire adopting the example of certain illustrious personages and, by discarding the razor, cultivate the stately beard. Apart from the brilliancy of the suggestion, the results in many cases would be bound to be startling.

King George V was crowned in June 1911. This cartoon makes the suggestion that all men should adopt a beard in his honour.
(Note: all newspaper pieces throughout this book are shown with the date above in a heading.)

A GUIDE TO THIS BOOK

The idea for this book arose from the National Archives' 1911 census website, which contains rich contextual and illustrative material relating to Dublin in that year, compiled by Paul Rouse and Mark Duncan.

The book starts in January with accounts of New Year celebrations, and proceeds month by month through the year. There are essays about Dublin in the early twentieth century on subjects like law and order, education, religion, transport, poverty, literary life and migration, among others. The essays are preceded by relevant reports from contemporary newspapers. In January, for example, a report on the theft of chalices from a church in Bray leads into a section on law and order. Other items of interest are whimsical, and the main news event was the visit of King George V and Queen Mary to Dublin in mid-July.

In contrast to the luxury of the royal visit coverage, there is a section on poverty in the city, illustrated by remarkable photographs from the Royal Society of Antiquaries' 'Darkest Dublin' collection. The section on fashion tells the story of the controversial 'trouser skirt', a peculiar garment in vogue at the time. The transport section reminds us that, long before the Luas, Dublin had a wonderful tram network, although the motor car was beginning its inexorable rise as the dominant transport choice.

Census forms are used to illustrate the household and institutional realities of life for Dublin citizens; for example, the page for Mountjoy Prison provides details of prisoners' crimes and length of sentences, as well as their occupations prior to imprisonment. Readers will see an invitation to a Mr and Mrs Alfred B. Coyle to at-tend a garden party at the vice-regal lodge during the royal visit (page 133); a quick search on the census website reveals Mr Coyle to be living at Highfield Road in Rathgar, an insurance broker, married for two years, with one child, also Alfred B.

The book does not purport to offer a comprehensive history of the year, rather to provide a series of interesting snapshots of what was happening. At the end of the book full references are supplied to enable readers to follow any trail that catches their imagination. It is hoped that readers will go on to use the census online (www.census.national archives.ie), as well as the variety of other sources provided in the book, to further research their own families, communities and neighbourhoods.

Postcard of O'Connell Bridge and Sackville Street.

INTRODUCTION

In 1911 Dublin was moving into a decade of remarkable change. The 1913 Lockout would redefine the nature of commerce and class relations in the city. The First World War would see many thousands of Dubliners fight at Gallipoli, Flanders and the Somme. Many would never come home. The 1916 Rising, followed by the War of Independence in 1919–21 and the ensuing Civil War, would change Ireland utterly.

Dublin was the centre of Irish administration, home to the lord lieutenant, the earl of Aberdeen and the chief secretary, Augustine Birrell, respectively the symbolic and administrative representatives of British power in Ireland. The city was also a transition destination for people emigrating, a port city and the location for large numbers of soldiers living in its many barracks. The population of the city and county of Dublin in 1911 was 477,196.

The Irish literary revival was in full swing, and many of its protagonists, Pádraig Pearse, Douglas Hyde, Augusta, Lady Gregory and W.B. Yeats lived and worked in the city. John Millington Synge had already seen some of his extraordinary plays produced in the newly founded Abbey Theatre, and had divided the city with his representation of the Irish peasantry. James Joyce was living abroad, but was already writing *Ulysses*, which, in probably the most important novel of the twentieth century, immortalised the city as it was in 1904. The Gaelic Athletic Association was attracting large numbers to its clubs and events.

Dublin was also home to some of the worst slums in Europe, with 33% of households living in single-room accommodation. The Georgian houses which formed the distinctive architectural fabric of the city had largely descended into multi-occupancy tenement dwellings. Diseases like typhoid, tuberculosis and dysentery were rife, and child mortality was extremely high. The middle classes had moved to the suburbs of Rathmines, Rathgar, Drumcondra and Clontarf, leaving the inner city to the poor.

Home Rule was the government of choice for the majority of Dubliners at this point, and the Irish Parliamentary Party, under the leadership of John Redmond, was the most powerful political party in the city. The outbreak of the First World War and the effect of the British response to the 1916 Rising were to scupper Home Rule and catapult separatist ideas into the ascendancy.

But no one foresaw any of this in 1911. We look back at the people who lived in the city then, in all of their economic, social, cultural, religious and ethnic diversity, and must remember that, like us today, they did not know what the future held for them. Like us, they wanted to live their lives in some degree of peace, comfort and affection, and to see their children live and prosper.

S1 M2 T3 W4 T5 F6 S7 ◗ S8 M9 T10 W11 T12 **F13** ○ S14 S15 M16 T17 W18 T19 F20 S21 ◖ **S22** M23 T24 W25 T26 F27 S28 S29 ● **M30**

Holidays and Observances

7…Old Christmas Day   8…First Quarter, 6.20am   14…Full Moon, 10.26pm   22…Last Quarter, 6.21am   30…New Moon, 9.45am

All
New Year
Joys be yours.

SUNDAY INDEPENDENT,
1 JANUARY 1911

CHIMING BELLS

NEW YEAR

RUNG IN;
THE OLD
RUNG OUT

LAST NIGHT IN DUBLIN

The New Year was ushered in last night in Dublin amid many manifestations of gaiety and rejoicing. With the advance of the age the manner of celebrating the passing away of the old year, and the birth of the new year, must necessarily undergo a transformation. In the "good old days," which generally means a time so far back that nobody remembers all its discomforts, New Year celebrations were, as a rule, associated with midnight orgies and scenes of disorder. The extraordinary escapades of the College students is now but a memory. In the present youthful generation, there is an entire absence of that dare-devil recklessness, which manifested itself in an utter disregard for the law, and its ministers.

So it was that last night the old time celebrations, which marked the dawning of the New Year, were noticeable by their absence. Even the usual turn out of the organ grinders in the Chancery lane district was not observed. This was always one of the features of the celebrations in Dublin, and large crowds flocked to the district to hear the extraordinary melodies of sound created by dozens of barrel organs.

SWEET CHIMING BELLS

The only link with the past characteristic of last night's rejoicings was the magnificent chime of bells at Christ Church. In accordance with a time-honoured custom, there was a great throng in the vicinity of the church, many of them indulging in the singing of New Year hymns. Several of the principal thoroughfares were crowded as midnight approached.

AT THE OPERA

It is pleasant to be able to chronicle that the Carl Rosa Opera Company season at the Theatre Royal has, so far, been crowned with unequivocal success. The houses have been good, the performances excellent, and, if encores afford any index, the popular appreciation of the keenest order.

* * * *

GAIETY THEATRE

"Robinson Crusoe" at the Gaiety has now got into full swing and promises to make a record so far as popularity is concerned. Few prettier pantomimes have ever been dressed at the Gaiety than the one which this year is drawing crowded houses nightly. Sparkling music, talented artistes, splendid scenery, beautiful dresses, and really good comedy and original specialties all contribute to make "Robinson Crusoe" one of the brightest productions seen in Dublin for many a year. The songs have caught the public fancy immensely and are more likely to do so as the days go by. Every facility is afforded not alone to people in the city but to those in the country to pay a visit to the pantomime, matinees taking place every Wednesday and Saturday. All who have not yet done so should make up their minds to go and see "Robinson Crusoe." Not alone to children, but to grown-ups it provides a treat.

* * * *

QUEEN'S THEATRE

"Little Red Riding Hood" at the Queen's continues to draw crowded and appreciative houses, and there is every sign that this welcome condition of affairs will continue. The popular taste was struck by a four weeks' pantomime production at the Brunswick street house, and the management are to be congratulated on their enterprise. The piece abounds in diverting fun. It may well be said that there is

5

not a dull moment from start to finish. This could hardly be otherwise with two such really clever comedians as Messrs. Cullen and Carthy to the forefront, assisted by Little Cluley. They are the life and soul of the piece, and their very names on the poster will ensure crowded audiences. In addition to the comedy of the pantomime – and there is plenty of it, and rightly so – the production is staged very prettily and attractively, and both scenery, effects, songs and specialities are excellent. Everything foreshows a successful production during the weeks yet to come. There will be matinees on Monday, January 2nd; Wednesday, January 4th, and Saturday, January 7th.

* * * *

EMPIRE THEATRE

At the Empire this week, the famous comedian, Harry Roxbury and his company in the laughing hit "The Prince of Monte Carlo" should prove a prime attraction. The piece is described as a merry musical melango with full comic opera chorus, and will be presented in three charming scenes. Another favourite turn will be that of Martin Henry and Irene Ross in the "Silver Medal." In a diversified programme the following also appears: Clark and Clare, the tramp and the girl; Warwick Chronicle of daily up-to-date events; Tambo and Tambo, the great tambourine spinners; the Two Ives, champion ball punchers; Edie Gray and boys, in a novel vocal and specialty act; Ida Dorrie, dainty comedienne, and the Empire Pictures. There will be a picture matinee at 2.30 daily during this week.

* * * *

ROTUNDA

The attractions of Carter's magic at the Round Room, Rotunda, during the week have attracted a full share of the public patronages during the holidays, there being full houses at each matinee and evening performance daily. The matinees have been remarkable for the good attendance experienced. In the perfect and elaborate series of illusions Mr. Carter has exhibited, all of which are excellently demonstrated, the most astonishing is clearly that styled "Levitation." In the opening part of the programme there are many skilful and smart digital manipulations, which are not only notable for their quickness and cleverness, but also for the pleasant run of wit, with which they are accompanied. This part includes an oracular future in the "Astral Hand," which indicates that answers to questions put by the audience. Miss Corinne Carter gives a clever performance in answering questions. "A Night in China" is a well presented Oriental act, which contains some surprises of an uncanny, but nevertheless pleasing character. The orchestra formed by the string band of the Rifle Brigade discourses popular music at each performance. There will be a matinee and evening entertainment all this week.

BEAN NA H-ÉIREANN
(WOMAN OF IRELAND)
VOL II, NO. 23, EANÁIR
(JANUARY) 1911

Na Fianna Éireann

The new year will bring new work, new energy, and new hope for the old cause, and we are all turning over the one idea in our hearts, "What can we do for Ireland in the new year?" 1911 must be a great year.

IRISH TIMES,
2 JANUARY 1911

New Year's Day in Dublin

On the stroke of midnight on Saturday the hoarse shrieks of steam "hooters" and syrens seemed almost to tear their way through the star-spangled empyrean, and the sweeter sounds of clanging and jangling bells from church towers tossed and jostled each other in joyous confusion as they welcomed the new and sped the parting year, while on foot the moving crowds of merry-makers exchanged their greetings and good wishes. Already the past is becoming but a memory: all hail the coming year with hope and confidence.

THE NEW YEAR

By contrast to the opening of last year, the incoming of 1911 is wholly free from excitement. Last January we were in the midst of election turmoil; now we have so recently emerged from another conflict that in affairs political an air of lassitude is everywhere observable. Two General Elections in the space of a year; the tragic interruption of the Constitutional struggle last May by the unexpected death of King Edward; the prolonged truce during which Ministers and ex-Ministers tried to arrange a settlement of one Veto question by consent; the collapse of the negotiations, and the decisive action of Mr. Asquith in appealing at once to the country, present a record as remarkable as can be chronicled of any year during the past half-century. Small wonder that the New Year should seem to come upon us almost unobserved. It was rumoured a while ago that the New Year's Honours List would give a foretaste of what the Peers might expect in case of an obstinate resistance to the passage of the Parliament Bill. From this point of view, the Honours List is a disappointment. No new Peers have been created. The most notable features of the British honours are the appointment of Mr. William Abraham, the son of a Welsh miner, as a member of the Privy Council, and the conferring of Knighthoods on a number of distinguished Civil Servants. Men prominent in the working of the Union of South Africa have also been honoured, and amongst them Dr. Jameson figures as the recipient of a baronetcy. In the Irish list the first name is that of Mr. T. Shillington, a veteran Liberal, who stood for South Armagh against the late Colonel Saunderson in 1885, and in South Tyrone as a Home rule candidate, against Mr. T.W. Russell in 1895. The Knighthood conferred on Dr. J.M. Redmond, a past president of the Royal College of Physicians, will give great pleasure, not only to his brethren of the medical profession, but to the wide public amongst whom his name and reputation are known. A similar distinction has been conferred on a leading member of the legal profession, Mr. J. P. Lynch, a past President of the Incorporated Law Society.

The figures of the Exchequer returns for the third quarter of the financial year also appear this morning, and they must be extremely gratifying to Mr. Lloyd George. In his statement last June, the Chancellor of the Exchequer estimated that the total revenue for the financial year would amount to £199,791,000, representing a total estimated increase of £68,094,544. To realise his estimate, Mr. Lloyd George must get in £61,850,368, but it cannot be doubted that this figure will be exceeded. Each of the past three quarters has yielded an increase over the corresponding quarter of the previous financial year, and these increases have taken place under every head of revenue except Crown Lands. The effects of the Budget are noticeable in the official returns of the shipments of whiskey from Dublin during 1910. At the end of September a comparison of the nine months' exports with those for the corresponding period of 1909 showed a decrease of 1,560 butts: the whole year's trade shows a decline of 1,290 butts. On the other hand, the shipments of porter from Dublin during the year have gone up by 76,645 hogsheads. We cannot discover from the Exchequer returns what is the proportion which Ireland contributes to the great increase in the Revenue; but it can be taken for granted that some of the calculations upon which Unionist journals have been basing statements about the insuperable financial obstacle to Home Rule would have to be recast were the figures fairly set forth. Apart, however, from the general question of the amount of increased taxation which Ireland has had to pay under the Budget, it is clear from the returns of the whiskey exports from Dublin during the last year that the distilling trade and the industries more or less dependent upon it have been badly hit. A decrease of more than 134,000 gallons in the shipments from this port tells its own story.

RINGING OUT THE OLD

Of the many time-honoured customs associated with the passing of the Old Year and the birth of the New in the Metropolis, the only one that seems to have survived is the ringing of the magnificent chime of the bells at Christchurch.

There were very many in the vicinity of the church awaiting the gladsome peal at midnight of Saturday. Light-hearted youths paraded the streets playing melodeons and mouth organs, and many persons among the crowds near the Church sang New Year hymns.

Shortly before midnight, as the bells pealed out merrily, the sirens of the boats in the harbour also welcomed the New Year.

Large numbers who flocked to the Chancery lane district to see the organ-grinders joining in the celebrations were disappointed.

BRAY
SACRILEGE

THE ACCUSED HOOTED IN COURT

Bray Courthouse was last evening a scene of great excitement in relation to a case which has caused widespread interest.

On the night of the 2nd and morning of the 3rd inst., St. Peter's Catholic Church, Bray, was broken into, and two chalices, and one ciborium stolen, and 15s in money taken out of donation boxes. Two brothers named William and Peter Fitzpatrick were arrested and charged with the offence. A spe-cial Court was held, over which Mr. Reigh, J.P., presided, to take depositions. On the way from the police barracks to the Court-house a hostile mob assembled and loudly hooted the prisoners, while there were cries of "Cowards," "Lynch them," "Hang them." The police had considerable difficulty in keeping the crowd from laying violent hands on the prisoners. In the Courthouse some two hundred men had assembled, and it was clear that they had gathered to make a demonstration.

POLICE EVIDENCE

When the prisoners were ar-raigned they denied all knowledge of the affair – at which declaration several people in the court hooted. George Meignean, clerk of St. Peter's, deposed to finding that a robbery had ☞

taken place. Sergeant Foley informed the Court that Peter Fitzpatrick had 5s 9d on him when arrested, and he could not say how he came by it. He was then drunk. On his becoming sober, he denied breaking into the chapel, and said he had got the money by begging. There was a cut on his chin – due, he said, to shaving, "but," added Sergeant Slater, who had preferred the charge, the man afterwards admitted that he had not shaved for three days. In Wm. Fitzpatrick's house, Sergeant Slator discovered the top of the missing ciborium and other articles. A remand for eight days was then granted.

At this stage the crowd in the body of the court made a rush in the direction of the prisoners, but the police held back those who wished to lay violent hands on the Fitzpatricks. There was a perfect yell of boohing, intermingled with persistent shouts of "Hang them," "Crucify them," "Murder them," "Shoot them," "Burn them," "We will kill them when we get them outside." Other language was also used. Inspector Hardy ordered the place to be cleared, which was done in a very quiet way by Sergeants Foley and Slator. The prisoners smiled at those who appeared disposed to attack them. The crowd remained outside the Courthouse until the prisoners were escorted to the police barracks, where they again had a hostile reception; but the police succeeded in getting them into the barracks without injury. A large number of people at the railway station hooted the prisoners as they left Bray for Dublin, where they are detained in Mountjoy Prison.

MURDER and SUICIDE in DUBLIN

Two occupants of the house, 9 Mary's Abbey, were found dead yesterday on the premises. They were William McKeon and his wife, Mrs. McKeown. The bodies were taken to Jervis street Hospital, and examined by Dr. O'Doherty, house surgeon. It was found that the woman's throat was cut right across, the wind-pipe being severed. Death had followed immediately upon the infliction of the wound. There was a similar cut across the man's throat. Both the deceased persons were between 30 and 40 years of age.

A cobbler's knife was found on the floor of the house, close to the bodies. The assumption made by the police from this, and from the results of their inquiries, is that William McKeon murdered his wife, and afterwards committed suicide, the cobbler's knife being used in each case. An extraordinary feature of the affair is suggested by the presence of blood on a grindstone in the room where the bodies lay. It would seem that after employing it on the woman, Mr. McKeon sharpened the knife on the stone before cutting his own throat.

LAW
&ORDER

Dublin Metropolitan Police constable, O'Connell Street.

Crime in Dublin tended to be more associated with petty theft than with violence. The city was notorious for its high levels of public drunkenness and its attendant disorder. In 1910 there were 2,462 charges of drunkenness in the Dublin Metropolitan police district, while a total of 3,758 people were drunk when they were taken into custody. The nature of crime in the city was consequently reflected in the make-up of the prison population.

The prisons of Dublin were home to hundreds of petty criminals, invariably from the poorer areas of the city, but Dublin was not regarded as particularly crime-ridden or dangerous. There was some serious crime, however, and the prison records reveal men in custody for indecent assault, conspiracy to extort money, shop-breaking, manslaughter and infanticide. Supplementing the prisons were juvenile reformatories, including one for young girls in Drumcondra at Grace Park Road.

Dublin was the headquarters for the Royal Irish Constabulary. The RIC was armed, wore military uniform, its constables lived in barracks across the country and were subject to military drill. The office of the inspector general was in Dublin Castle, and its principal depot was in the Phoenix Park.

The Four Courts in Dublin in 1911 was the site of the Supreme Court of Judicature, which included the High Court of Justice of Ireland and the Court of Appeal. The lawyers who worked in the courts had increasingly moved to the suburbs, but a significant number still lived in the Georgian streets and squares of the city centre.

The primary law enforcement agency in the city was the Dublin Metropolitan Police, which was established in 1836 and operated under the control of central government. Unlike the RIC, its members were not armed and officers were generally recruited from the ranks.

In 1911 the majority of policemen were farmers' sons, many of whom had an uneasy relationship with certain sections of the city's inhabitants. This unease darkened into full-blown hostility following perceptions of police brutality during the 1913 Lockout. Among other incidents, the police baton-charged strikers along Sackville Street (now O'Connell Street) and killed two men in the process.

As well as its regular officers, the Metropolitan Police also had an intelligence-gathering unit of detectives, G Division. This division had been centrally involved in undermining the Fenians in 1867, and in 1911 continued to play a major role in investigating political and subversive activity in the city. Among the places in which G Division took a considerable interest was the newsagent's shop owned by IRB man Tom Clarke at the corner of Great Britain Street and Sackville Street (now Parnell and O'Connell Streets, respectively).

The activities of political subversives were not nearly as pervasive in city life as was the presence of prostitutes. Typical of any city with a large garrison, prostitution was a thriving business in Dublin. Brothels or 'kip-houses'

DEEDS THAT WON THE EMPIRE
THE CAPTURE OF THE POLES.

DEEDS THAT WON THE EMPIRE
The capture of the poles

This postcard relates to an event in Dublin during the preparations for the king's visit in July 1911.
Printed in green font on the back was: 'The poles that once in Grafton Street / Their tales of treason told / Now lie confined in close retreat / In Dublin Castle's hold. / Victorious are the brave blue coats; The rebels reign is o'er. The Union Jack serenely floats; The Empire's safe once more'.

It refers to the dismantling of poles (and a banner) in June 1911 which had been erected in Grafton Street by the Independent United National Societies Committee in protest of the forthcoming visit of George V and Queen Mary.

The poles bore a banner which on one side had the announcement: 'Do not miss the great independence demonstration at Beresford Place, Thursday evening, 7.30 pm' and on the other side: 'Awaken thy courage, O Ireland' and (in Irish) 'Thou art not conquered yet, dear land'.

as they were known locally were an established feature of life in tenement areas. The 'Monto' district (named after Montgomery Street, now Foley Street) around Gloucester Street was the best-known area for prostitution, but there were also well-known brothels around the docks and in the south inner city.

Prostitutes also had regular standings in areas such as Grafton Street, St Stephen's Green, Sackville Street and Harcourt Street. Respectable women avoided walking down one side of Sackville Street. Protestant and Catholic organisations frequently attempted to close down brothels in the city and ran a number of Magdalen asylums intended to 'save' or 'reform' women who worked on the streets. They had only limited success in closures; we now know that street life may have been preferable.

The women who worked in the brothels and on the streets were believed to be country girls who had fallen on hard times in the city, while the brothel owners or 'madams' were known to be local women. For all the condemnation of their occupation, the women were generally considered to be decent and kind, forced through circumstance into an unfortunate life on the streets. Quite a number ended up in penitentiaries as well as in Mountjoy Prison.

In 1911 there were thousands of troops living in Dublin in at least eight barracks across the city. At Richmond Barracks in Inchicore there were 1,600 soldiers, a hospital for 100 patients, officer accommodation and stabling for 25 horses. At Portobello Barracks in Rathmines there was extensive room for cavalry units, a garrison church and a canteen. Wellington Barracks on the South Circular Road had been built as a prison in 1813 but, by 1911, was operating as a barracks. The largest barracks was the Royal Barracks (now the National Museum of Ireland) at Benburb Street. The Barracks had had its central portion, Royal Square, laid out in 1701 and by 1735 it could house five battalions, comprising around 5,000 men. Further squares were added over time and the Royal Barracks became the heart of the British military operation in Ireland.

Many of the soldiers stationed in these barracks were English, Scottish and Welsh, but others were locals. Irish soldiers made up a considerable section of the British Army. Recruiting sergeants and reservists lived in ordinary houses across the city.

Around 130,000 Irishmen had fought in the Napoleonic Wars and in the 1830s more than 40% of the British Army was Irish. By 1899 this percentage had fallen to 13% (higher than the 9% Irish share of the overall population of the United Kingdom) and it would appear that rising nationalist sentiment undermined army recruitment in the first decade of the twentieth century. Poverty made enlistment an attractive option, and approximately 200,000 Irishmen served in the British armed forces during the First World War. ❀

DUBLINERS IN EXILE

Here James Joyce writes to his brother Stanislaus about the delay in publication of his book *Dubliners*. He left Ireland in 1904 and, apart from four visits up to 1912, was never to live in Ireland again. Although Joyce's exile was self-imposed, many left by the Kingston Ferry never to return. The postcard reads: 'Barriera Vecchia 32. It may interest you to hear that *Dubliners*, announced for publication for the third time yesterday 20 January, is again postponed *sine die* and without a word of explanation. I know the name and tradition of my country too well to be surprised at receiving three scrawled lines in return for five years of constant service to my art and constant waiting and indifference and disloyalty in return for the 150,000 francs of continental money which I have deflected into the pockets of hungry Irishmen and women since they drove me out of their hospitable bog six years ago. Jim. 22.1.911'.

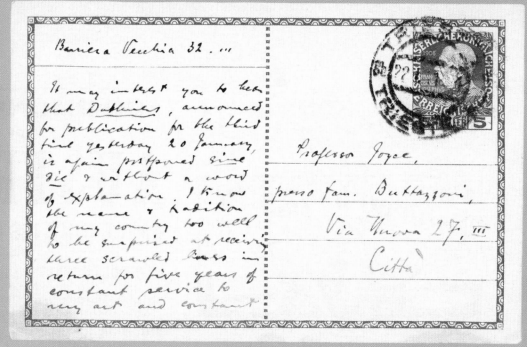

BEAN NA H-ÉIREANN
(WOMAN OF IRELAND)
VOL II, NO. 23, EANÁIR (JANUARY) 1911

While emigration is being so loudly advocated by England and her agents in this country, some of her own Radical papers are busily engaged in publishing the horrors and miseries of "Canada's death trap". For unskilled workers without capital the outlook is very black indeed. A dollar (4s. 2d) out there does not go further than a shilling at home. Rent is higher; the cost of living and of the necessities of life are much dearer than they are at home, while the severity of the climate necessitates better fires, better clothes, and better food.

Emigration
& Migration

In 1911 there were more than 80 cross-channel sailings per week to Britain from Dublin port. Many of the sailings carried emigrants leaving a country and a city unable to offer a basic living. Some were Dubliners, but many were from the Irish countryside, passing through the city since there was no work available to them. Dubliners traditionally emigrated in fewer numbers than those from rural areas. Between 1891 and 1901, 430,393 people emigrated from Ireland; only 9,487 of these were from Dublin. Dublin, alone among Irish counties, enjoyed a small increase in total population in the second half of the nineteenth century.

There is clear evidence that the number of people from rural areas living in Dublin was remarkably low, particularly in comparison to the inward migration experienced by other cities of similar size in the United Kingdom. Less than 10% of all migration undertaken by Irish people ended in Dublin. In many respects this was related to the stagnation of the city's economy. Dublin was unable to absorb the hundreds of thousands who left the land every decade.

Those who did come from the country generally came from the surrounding counties of Meath, Kildare and Wicklow, or other eastern counties like Wexford, with only 7% of migrants living in Dublin in 1911 coming from Connacht. Shopkeepers and publicans, a high proportion of whom were from the country, often chose to employ people who came from the same area as themselves. For example, the majority of people who worked in the shops and pubs of Talbot Street in 1911 were born in the same county as the owners.

Those who did not live in the shops and pubs, or in boarding houses, often lived with relatives, neighbours or work colleagues who had come to Dublin before them. The extent to which Dublin was primarily a city for native Dubliners is also emphasised by the number of boarding houses that were filled with Dubliners, including a nineteen-room boarding house on Church Street, 108 of whose 114 lodgers had been born in Dublin.

The hotels in the city offer a valuable insight into the people who lived and worked in Dublin, as well as those who travelled there. The Shelbourne Hotel on St Stephen's Green was one of the most prestigious in the city, and its staff was truly cosmopolitan. Although many who worked as cooks and chambermaids were Irish, the waiting staff comprised eight Germans, three Austrians, and one each from Bohemia and England. They all lived together in a house near the hotel on Kildare Street and, on the outbreak of the First World War, the German staff was interned.

Many of the servants employed in Dublin houses were from rural areas. In certain areas country people accounted for three-quarters of the servants employed. Some businesses, including the Guinness brewery and the canal companies, employed country people ahead of Dubliners, because they tended to be larger and stronger and more accustomed to heavy lifting work. Dubliners, however, were not generally displaced by unskilled rural migrants. For example, city centre tenement streets such as Mabbot Street and Tyrone Street were home to Dublin-born labourers who accounted for almost 90% of inhabitants.

The level of country migrants living in the city peaked at times when the rural economy faltered or collapsed. The devastation of famine in the 1840s brought starving victims to the city in search of relief. So did intermittent agricultural depression, such as that of 1879 to 1881 when the city's workhouses, like the South Dublin Union at James's Street, were filled with rural dwellers. That most rural people used Dublin merely as a staging post for emigration is confirmed by the fact that, in 1911, more than 70% of the city's population had been born there.

Native Dubliners were convinced that the city was being overrun by country people and foreigners, and were particularly devoted to the notion that migrants were displacing them in employment. This was despite evidence to the contrary, although people did come to Dublin to seek work from cities like Glasgow, Liverpool and Birmingham.

Delusions of foreign invasion also surfaced in political debate. In March 1907, a speaker at a Dublin Corporation meeting complained that the Hammond Lane Foundry employed 'only Scotsmen and niggers'. In reply the manager pointed out that the workforce was comprised of 87 Irishmen, fifteen Scots and one American, and that the employment of the foreigners was due to the lack of specialist skills in the local labour market.

Foundries, mills, engineering and electrical firms regularly brought skilled labour to Dublin. Indeed, about 25% of all migrants to Dublin were born outside Ireland. Children returned with their migrant parents, others married Irish men and women, still more came to work. They came from near and far: Corfu, Jamaica, Hungary, China, France, Rhodesia and, of course, America.

Neighbourhoods such as Kingstown and Rathmines had high percentages of non-Dublin residents. Their children were often taught by teachers, many of them women, who had themselves come from England, France or even South America. Schools, too, drew in their quota of foreign children to live and study as boarders.

Many of the migrants who came to the city were not Catholics. The most recent wave of migrants, members of the Jewish faith, like the Jacobsons of Camden Street, had come from Eastern Europe in the preceding decades and made Dublin their home. They established a thriving community in the south inner city, in the streets around the South Circular Road, and soon offered a flourishing contribution to life in Dublin. ❄

MIXED MARRIAGES

THE PAPAL DECREE

PROTEST BY PROTESTANTS

Archbishop Peacocke presided at a large meeting in the Metropolitan Hall last night, when resolutions were passed protesting against the Papal Decree "Ne Temere" on the subject of mixed marriages, and calling upon the Government to take action in the matter.

The Decree, Archbishop Peacocke said, was not enforced in Germany, and it would be for the public peace of Ireland that a similar exemption were conceded.

The dividing wall between Protestants and their Catholic fellow-countrymen was high enough already, and they should not want to make it higher.

During the speech by Mr. J. H. Campbell, K.C., M.P., the Executive Government and the Viceroy's name were groaned.

A number of letters were received from prelates of the Church of Ireland sympathising with the object of the meeting.

CHURCHMEN'S VIEWS

Apologies for absence were received from Most Rev. Dr Keene, the Right Rev. Dr. Archdall, Dean Bernard, the Ven. Robert Walsh, Sir Algernon Coote, and Mr. A.L. Horner, K.C., M.P., etc.

The Right Rev. Dr. Chadwick wrote stating that the manner in which the Decree was being worked constituted a most serious attack upon the rights of free Irish citizens.

The Right Rev. Fr. D'Arcy wrote urging that the matter should be forced upon the attention of the Government and the country.

The Right Rev. Dr. Elliott in the course of a letter said: "If the Nationalists wish to convince us of their impartial action under Home Rule they should hold a meeting repudiating the Decree, or at least requesting the Pope to withdraw it. It may fairly be made a test of the toleration which Mr. Redmond promises to Protestants."

The Right Rev. Dr. O'Hara wrote referring to the Decree as "cruel and intolerant," and the Right Rev. Dr. Meade wrote sympathising with the movement.

THE CHAIRMAN'S ADDRESS

The Chairman said that they were there to protest against the action of the Catholic Church in promulgating a Decree according to which any marriage between a Protestant and Catholic was not valid. The law upon which the Decree was founded was adopted at the Council of Trent in the year 1563, but there was a provision then made that it was not to be operative in any country or parish unless it had been promulgated therein.

DID NOT WANT MIXED MARRIAGES

"We don't want mixed marriages," added his Grace. "We do our best as far as we can to prevent them, but when they do take place, I protest against the Decree which seeks to nullify those marriages on the sole ground that certain conditions laid down by the Church of Rome have not been fulfilled, which conditions they enforce in Ireland, but do not enforce in Germany."

It would be for the public peace and tranquillity of this country if the exemption given to Germany were conceded to Ireland.

There was applause when he concluded by saying that the dividing wall between Protestants and their Catholic fellow-countrymen was high enough, and they did not want to make it higher.

The Moderator of the General Assembly (Rev. Dr. Murphy) proposed a resolution protesting against the Decree. There was much applause when he said they could not allow their people to be taken from them. It would be well for the country if all the old animosities were forgotten, but how could that be as long as events of that kind happened.

The resolution was seconded by Mr. J.H. Campbell, K.C., M.P., who said they were there to protest as freemen against an act of intolerable aggression on the part of a foreign power (applause) as well as to resent an attempt to strike a blow at the very heart of their social and domestic life (renewed applause).

THE CASE OF MRS. McCANN

Referring to the case of Mrs. McCann in Belfast, he said, amid applause, that as long as he was spared he would fight the battle of this case.

A reference by Mr. Campbell to an appeal to the Executive evoked boohs for the Executive, and the Lord Lieutenant's name was loudly groaned. He asked why were the voices of Mr. Swift MacNeill, Mr. Joseph Devlin, or Mr. John Redmond (groans) silent with regard to the Papal Decree and Mrs. McCann.

A collection was then made to defray the expenses of the meeting, the balance to be sent to Mrs. McCann.

The Rev. Dr. Prenter moved a resolution calling upon the Government to take such action as would secure to those who had been married according to the law of the land freedom from interference from clergymen or others that might lead to a violation of the marriage contract.

Why did not Mr. John Redmond convene a meeting of protest in the Mansion House, and why did not Mr. Wm. O'Brien, out of the wealth of his vocabulary, characterise, as only he could, the conduct of his own Church in this matter.

The Very Rev. Dr. Leatham seconded the resolution, which was carried, and the Rev. Chancellor O'Connor, M.A., proposed that copies of the resolutions should be forwarded to the lord lieutenant.

MEETING AND VICEROY

At this stage there was much groaning whereupon the speaker said - "The Lord Lieutenant is the King's representative. I have great respect for the Lord and Lady Aberdeen, although I may not agree with them in some things."

The resolution also provided that the resolutions should be sent to the Prime Minister, the Chief Secretary, and Mr. A.J. Balfour.

This was seconded by Rev. R. W. Budd, and supported by Rev. Wm. Corkey, M.A. (Belfast).

A vote of thanks to Archbishop Peacocke was passed, on the motion of Captain Wade Thompson, seconded by Mr. James Chambors, K.C., M.P.

An overflow meeting was in progress while the meeting in the large hall was being held.

RELIGION

Religious divides in Dublin in the early twentieth century were rarely marked by violence, unlike in Belfast. Sectarianism among Dubliners was more nuanced, more inclined towards implicit understandings of distinctiveness, but religion was a defining presence in city life. In 1911 the city was 83% Catholic, 13% Church of Ireland, 2% Presbyterian and Methodist and 2% 'others', which included a growing Jewish presence.

The range of religions represented in the city was wide. There were theosophists and Baptists, Evangelists, Plymouth Brethren, Episcopalians, members of the Salvation Army, people who refused to disclose their religion or proclaimed to have none, including those known as 'free-thinkers', agnostics and Independent Christians.

There was a tendency among minority religions to cluster together. Presbyterians and Methodists accounted for almost one-tenth of the population of Clontarf. Similarly, there was a large Jewish community around the South Circular Road.

Generally, Protestants were more prominent in various suburbs of the city, such as Monkstown, where Catholics comprised a minority of the population. Protestant religious infrastructure included an Orange Hall at York Road in Kingstown.

There were boarding houses and hotels which were clearly run along sectarian lines, but the census reveals that the great majority were of mixed creed. All across the city there were marriages ☞

between people of different faiths, people bringing up children in different faiths and people employing servants of various faiths.

The diversity of certain streets was as striking as the uniformity of those in which one creed or the other dominated. Oaklands Park in Pembroke was home to Catholics, Protestants, Presbyterians, Methodists, Wesleyans, Baptists, 'independents' and individuals who refused to disclose their religion. Closer to the city centre, Harcourt Street was also a place of religious diversity.

At the head of the Catholic Church in the city was the archbishop of Dublin, William Walsh, a strong nationalist whose politics were more inclined towards Sinn Féin than the Irish Parliamentary Party, and who was the first chancellor of the National University of Ireland. There were many religious orders in the city. The Dublin diocesan seminary was based at Clonliffe Road; the Vincentians were based at All Hallows at Gracepark Road, Drumcondra;

the Jesuits at Milltown and the Holy Ghost Fathers at Kimmage. Priests and Christian Brothers were also heavily involved in education in the city.

Orders of nuns ran national schools, exclusive boarding schools, homes for the aged and the destitute, and established hospitals. The Sisters of Charity ran St Vincent's hospital and Magdalene asylums, and the contemplative Carmelites had convents and churches in Dublin. Personal piety, a product of the nineteenth-century devotional revolution, continued to impact on the city in 1911. Dubliner Frank Duff was later inspired by Marian piety to establish the Legion of Mary in 1921. Reformed alcoholic Matt Talbot lived with his mother at Rutland Street and lived a devotional life.

The Church of Ireland formed the largest minority in the city and had a formidable network of churches, schools and hospitals across the city. In the decades before 1911, Protestant domination of the higher professions was steadily eroded by the emergence

of an educated Catholic elite. Nonetheless, in law, medicine, the civil service and the upper ranks of the army, Protestants were substantially over-represented. There is clear evidence that certain trades were associated with certain religions. Coopering was dominated by Catholic workers, while the city's growing electrical industry was staffed by Protestants, many of whom had arrived from England.

There was a growing feeling of isolation among the capital's Protestant and unionist elite, for so long the dominant power in the city. Nationalists had taken charge of Dublin Corporation and, although their militancy was largely rhetorical, the sense of rising nationalist fervour was strong. There were constant Catholic concerns at what was perceived as proselytising by Protestants. Attempts by Protestants to improve social welfare provision in the city, such as the Church of Ireland social services union fund for elderly women, were often criticised as being driven by ulterior motives.

Cardinal Logue, King George V and Queen Mary
lead others from one of Maynooth's buildings.

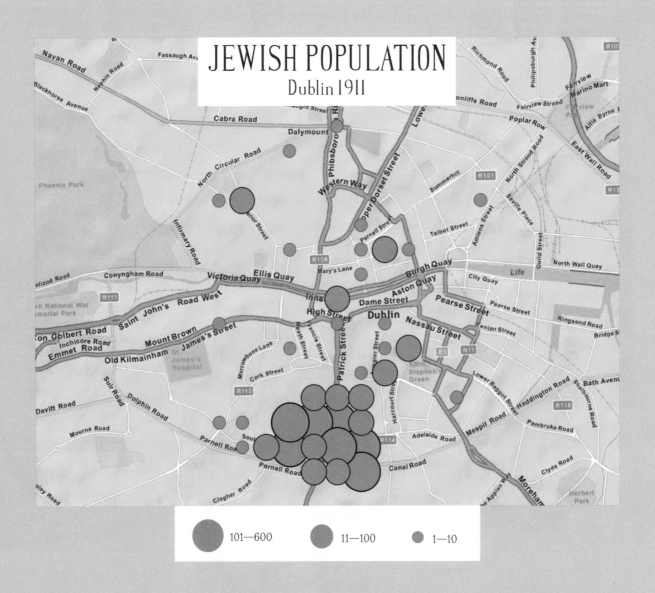

JEWISH POPULATION
Dublin 1911

101—600   11—100   1—10

The census return made in April 1911 shows that most of the small Jewish population
was concentrated in the Portobello area of the city.

It was such fears which drove the Catholic hierarchy to reject any notion of non-denominational education in the city, whether at national, secondary or university level. Prestigious fee-paying schools such as Blackrock College for Catholics, Monkstown Park and Alexandra College for Protestants, and Wesley College for Methodists, emphasised the divide. Ultimately, though, students from these schools were destined for similar careers in the professions, or in the public service across the British Empire.

In 1911 there were several thousand Jews in Dublin, mostly based around Portobello and the South Circular Road. Many were immigrants from Eastern Europe, including Poland (see return for the Solomon family of Pleasant Street) and Russia, where they had fled the pogroms of Tsar Alexander II. Others were Jewish immigrants from Britain and established themselves as dentists and surgeons. They built synagogues and schools, while other Jewish institutions established in the area included a hebra at No. 52 Camden Street, one of six in the Portobello area, formed for religious and charitable purposes as a transitional place for Jewish immigrants adapting to life in Dublin.

Quakers—the Society of Friends—had been present in Dublin from the 1650s. From modest beginnings, they had evolved into an often wealthy community of industrialists and entrepreneurs, distinguished by their philanthropy. Among the most prominent Quaker families in Dublin were the Jacobs, who owned the substantial confectionery business, and the Bewleys of Kerrymount, biscuit makers and tea and coffee merchants who owned thriving Oriental-style cafes in the city. ❊

W1 T2 F3 S4 S5 ◖ M6 T7 W8 T9 F10 S11 S12 ○ M13 T14 W15 T16 F17 S18 S19 M20 ◗ T21 W22 T23 F24 S25 S26 M27 T28

Holidays and Observances

2…Candlemas Day   6…First Quarter, 3.28pm   8…Half-Quarter Day   13…Full Moon, 10.38am

14…St Valentine   15…Old Candlemas Day   21…Last Quarter, 3.44am   28…Shrove Tuesday

IRISH INDEPENDENT,
22 FEBRUARY 1911

FARTHEST SOUTH
SIR E. SHACKLETON'S
LECTURE

The Lord Lieutenant and the Countess of Aberdeen honoured the renowned Irish explorer, Sir Ernest Shackleton, by their presence amongst the very large and appreciative audience that assembled in the Round Room, Rotunda, last night to hear him describe his recent voyage of discovery to the South Pole. The lecture was illustrated by a number of lantern slides from photographs taken during the trip, and also by a splendid series of cinematograph pictures made on the expedition.

After telling some of the difficulties and hardships encountered in the dash for the South Pole, the lecturer said that on that very day two years ago he and his companions were dragging their way on the return journey to the Nimrod through a howling blizzard, wet, weak, half-frozen and famished for want of food. He remembered noting in his diary, "Food lies ahead, and death stalks us from behind." In the supreme attempt they had been trudging for months on a meal a day, and every biscuit was hoarded to the veriest crumb. Each morning, before taking their scanty rations, they deluded themselves like children by picturing for each other the most extravagant and voluptuous feasts in a vain effort to forget their misery.

Besides reaching furthest South, they established other records. The record they felt most thankful for, however, was the fact that they were the first South Polar party to return to civilisation without the loss of a single man (applause). There was one interesting feature of the trip which he had not told at his first lecture in Dublin. That was, that none of the men were ever troubled with a cold, except on one occasion, when they had been many months sledging through the intensely cold ice and snow, and a bale of clothing was opened which let loose the germs.

Many humorous incidents were recounted. Professor David, of Sydney University, was so extra polite that once, when he had fallen down a chasm, he courteously called out to his comrades, "If you are not too busy, I may say I'm down a chasm and want to get up." Pointing to the serio-comic antics of the penguins as they waddled on the screen pictures, the lecturer casually said that the hobble skirt had evidently been fashionable in the Antarctic long before it was known further North.

A choice concert programme was contributed to by Miss K. Hayes, Miss L. Christie, Messrs. D. Jones and J. C. Doyle, Madame Lucy Donnelly accompanying.

Irish explorer Tom Crean sits on a loaded sledge. Teddy Evans stands beside. In 1911 these two men were on a rival expedition (British Antarctic Expedition, 1910–13), led by Robert Falcon Scott.

THE HAREM-SCAREM SKIRT

Paris has been flirting for some time past with the idea of a divided feminine garment; but the pictures of the new harem skirt which have appeared in some of the London papers will not help to make it popular. Its very name suggests what it is, a sort of mongrel adaptation of the garment worn by Turkish women, and although it is described as being "sensible, hygenic, graceful and unrivalled for comfort and elegance," it is far from possessing all these advantages. More than anything else, it resembles the costume of the circus clown which is intended to look grotesque and absurd, and by no possible stretch of the imagination could it be called a thing of beauty and elegance. Fashion has gone to many extremes, from the days of the crinoline to those of the hobble-skirt, but it would be ridiculous to speak of this freak as a new fashion. If it survives its birth, it will be known as the harem-scarem skirt but it is doubtful if it will reach the christening stage of its brief and inglorious life.

'Shocked gentleman on Hampstead Heath' by Jack B. Yeats.

THE TROUSER SKIRT

PARISIAN AUDIENCE LAUGHS IT OFF THE STAGE

Telegraphing on Sunday, the Paris correspondent of the London Daily Express says – The opinion of the Paris public on the trouser skirt was expressed unhesitatingly yesterday afternoon at the Comedie Francaise during the dress rehearsal of "After Me," the new play by Henry Bernstein, author of "The Thief." When the curtain rose on the first act Mlle. Provost, one of the prettiest actresses in Paris, was seen to be in an arm chair and puffing gently at a cigarette. She put her feet upon a stool in front of her, and the house rocked with laughter. Mlle. Provost wore a trouser skirt. Every time the trouser skirt came into view the audience laughed, and if the play had not proved such a strong one as it did, the dressmaker's freak would have wrecked it.

THE TROUSER SKIRT

AMUSING RUMOUR IN PARIS

An amusing rumour is current in Paris that a number of well-known women are determined to force the hands of the police authorities and make them prohibit the wearing of the trouser skirt in public. They will do this, says the Paris correspondent of the "Daily

Express," London, by appearing in public in trousers of the usual men's cut.

The wearing of men's attire by women and of women's attire by men is a legal offence in France, except at Carnival time. The police, therefore, would be obliged to arrest the women wearing trousers. These would immediately protest against their arrest unless the wearers of trouser skirts be made liable to arrest as well, for the law says nothing about the form of trousers which are illegal dress for women.

TROUSER SKIRT IN BERLIN

HAREM SKIRTS IN SPAIN

RIOTOUS SCENES

The Berlin Correspondent of the Daily News, telegraphing on Tuesday, says – The ladies' tailors here are overwhelmed with inquiries about the trouser skirt as a consequence of its first appearance on the Berlin stage last Sunday. According to the Press, several hundred orders for the new skirt have already been given. German women refuse to adopt the more extravagant forms of the Paris mode. The outer robe is only slightly slashed at the side, hardly revealing the trousers beneath. The first women to appear in the Berlin streets in a trouser skirt declared that it was very convenient for walking. A lady dressed in the new fashion was mobbed at Cologne yesterday.

The Madrid correspondent of the Daily Telegraph, telegraphing on Tuesday, says – The harem skirt continues to cause public scandals. Yesterday in Valencia three young women ventured into the street, and the tumult occasioned was so great that over four thousand persons surrounded them, pursuing them mercilessly, and even wishing to deprive them of the offensive garments. Many police men were obliged to intervene with the object of protecting the ladies, who were taken to the police station, and charged with creating a scandal in the public highway. To-day in Madrid another incident took place in the Puerta del Sol, and the police were called upon to protect an elderly lady who was wearing a "jupe-culette."

"HAREM" SKIRT

THE FREAK IN DUBLIN

The "harem" skirt has arrived in Dublin, but opinion among fashionable costumers and dressmakers is divided, like the garment itself, as to whether it shall become popular. The hope of commonsense persons, however, is that this latest freak of fashion, which has called forth general ridicule wherever it has made its appearance, will not be adopted by Irishwomen.

A lady wearing a "harem" skirt paraded Grafton St on Monday and Tuesday. She is a model in one of the smartest modistes' establishments in the city, and the exhibition has made for the purpose of eliciting the feelings of the people in the metropolis with regard to the freakish innovation.

Clery's
Great Summer Sale.

Bargains in Millinery
and
Feather Stoles.

In view of an Early Millinery greatly for New

Autumn Season all reduced to prepare Stocks.

Straw Hat, in all shades.
Trimmed Roses.
Usual Price, 15/9
Sale Price, 12/9

Feather Stoles in all colors.
Sale Prices
from 8/11.

Straw Hat for young girl.
Trimmed Pink Roses and Foliage.
Usual Price, 8/11.
Sale Price, 6/11.

HATS MADE TO ORDER ARE NOT RETURNABLE.   MILLINERY IS NOT SENT ON APPROBATION.

Clery & Co., Ltd.,   Dublin.

In Dublin in 1911, most women had their clothes made by dressmakers, of whom there were over 3,000 in the city and county. Women would buy bolts of material from drapery stores, and have them made to a pattern by their local dressmaker. It's clear from the controversy about trouser-skirts that department stores like Arnott's, Clery's, Switzer's and Brown Thomas were playing a part in leading-edge fashion, but dressmakers attempted to emulate the latest looks, like the 'Gibson Girl' sporty outfits made popular in the United States, and the Edwardian 'tailor-made' suits, deemed ideal for travelling.

A corner dressmaker could make a dress based on a magazine picture for between five and six shillings. On the other hand, a fully embellished ball gown could cost up to 80 guineas from a superior establishment, which would have used sweated labour to sew on the innumerable sequins and beads.

Most women wore long knickers, a chemise and a highly constricting corset or stays, designed to achieve a tiny waist. Over these was worn a petticoat, a dress or blouse and skirt, a coat or mantle, and a hat (there were almost 600 milliners in Dublin in 1911). The Edwardian silhouette emulated the long, slim model favoured by the French designer, Paul Poiret, involving an extra-long corset and probable agony for its wearers. The abandonment of the corset was seen as a sign of advanced feminist views, and not ladylike.

Beautifully embellished ornate blouses were worn by every class. Home dressmakers did their best to emulate the fussy couture blouses, using fine pin tucks, embroidery, appliqué, insertions of lace, faggoting, pleats and lace trim. ☞

Original lace blouse pattern from
Irish Industries, Dublin.

After the slimmer silhouette arrived, hats grew wider, with lavish trims often sticking out well beyond the brim. The hats were named Merry Widow hats after the popular operetta of the era. Feathers were used extensively as decoration on the hats and as boas. The fur skins of whole animals such as foxes were used as wraps about the shoulders. Washable kid gloves were worn with outdoor garments in both winter and summer. Fancy gloves were also in vogue, made in suede and silk and covered with fine embroidery.

Parasols were still used as accessories and in summer they dripped with lace and added to the overall image of stylised prettiness. Handbags were not fashionable, but small decorative bags with a dainty strap that hung from the wrist were sometimes used. Well-off women carried little money as goods were charged to accounts, and only minimal make-up was usual, so none was carried.

THE "MERRY WIDOW"

Regular Price,

14s. - 6d.

SALE do.,

12/9.

LADIES' BLACK GLACE KID BOOTS.
Patent or Self Cap.

Ready-to-Wear Clothing Bargains.

This Season's Styles in all the Fashionable Patterns of Good Serviceable Materials. Clothes that will give you satisfaction and add to our good reputation.

School Outfits a Specialitie.

"Whitby" Suit for boys,
8 to 13 years.
Regular Prices,
12s. 6d., 17s. 6d., 25s.
SALE do.,
9s. 6d., 12s. 6d., 19s. 6d.

Youths' Suit, with Breeches or Knickers, in Tweeds and Serges
Regular Prices,
18s. 6d., 25s., 37s. 6d.
SALE do.,
12s. 6d., 19s. 6d., 29s. 6d.

Gent's Suits, in best Irish Tweeds and Serges,
Regular Prices,
35s., 45s., 55s.
SALE do.,
29s. 6d., 39s. 6d., 47s. 6d.

Youths' D.B. Overcoat, with or without Strap at back.
In Smart Tweeds.
Regular Prices,
29s. 6d., 37s. 6d., 47s. 6d.
SALE do.,
22s. 6d., 30s. 6d., 39s. 6d.

"Sackville" Overcoat,
For Boys 4 to 13 years.
Regular Prices,
14s. 6d., 19s. 6d., 29s. 6d.
SALE do.,
11s. 6d., 15s. 6d., 22s. 6d

D.B. Overcoat, with or without Strap.
Regular Prices,
35s. to 75s.
SALE do.,
29s. 6d. to 65s.

☛ In *Privileged lives: a social history of middle-class Ireland 1882–1989*, Tony Farmar outlines what men used to wear in 1911: 'A suit was *de rigueur*, with a waistcoat, completed with boots and a watch-chain, and a long-tailed shirt (with detachable collar), a tie, and long underwear'. Flannel suits cost between 10 and 21 shillings, and Irish tweed suits between 22 and 35 shillings. For sporting occasions, a jacket and trousers could be worn. Knee-breeches were popularised by Douglas Hyde, and favoured by Gaelic League members. ❧

Switzer and Co., Ltd., have just received some of
the new season's model corsets. No. 362 (as illustration) is a charming model made of strong white
coutille with low bust and very long over the hips.

MILLINERY

Soft Flexible Chip, Trimmed Velvet.   In all
self colours and putty, and new burnt
trimmed, all shades, 5/11

MANSFIELD SISTERS

THE RECOGNISED MILLINERS,

28 Wicklow Street.

WINTER GOWNS.

RECEPTION

DRESSES

AND

SMART

MILLINERY

IN THE

Latest Modes.

AT

La Maison Claire,
4 Grafton Street.

Inspection Invited. Model Gowns and Costumes.

● W1 T2 F3 S4 S5 M6 ◗ T7 W8 T9 F10 S11 S12 M13 ○ T14 W15 T16 F17 S18 S19 M20 T21 W22 ◖ T23 F24 S25 S26 M27 T28 W29 ● T30 F31

Holidays and Observances

1…Ash Wednesday. New Moon, 0.31am   7…First Quarter, 11.20pm   14…Full Moon 11.59pm   17…St Patrick's Day

21…Spring commences 5.54pm   23…Last Quarter, 0.26am   30…New Moon, 0.38pm

MISS HORNIMAN'S WITHDRAWAL

THE DIRECTORS OF THE NATIONAL THEATRE SOCIETY

-to

WHITNEY and MOORE, Solicitors, Dr.

C O S T S

as between Solicitor and Client including costs of and incidental to preparation and completion of Deed of Release
also of and incidental to preparation
and completion of Deed declaring trusts
also of and incidental to incorporation
of The National Theatre Society Limited
and preparation and completion of deed
dissolving the old Society also of Deed
in connection with preparing Memorial to
His Excellency the Lord Lieutenant of
Ireland and of application for a Patent
for "The National Theatre Society Limited"
also of and in connection with preparation and completion of Agreement dated
10th March 1911.

Mr. Joseph MacDermott 　　　1st part Miss Horniman 2nd part Mr. David F. Moore 　　　3rd part	COSTS of & incidental to preparation and com- pletion of Deed of Release herein and proposed Release from Mechanics Institute

1910

Febr. 17 Attg. Mr. Yeats on his call. He instructed

1

Reproduced to the left is the first page of the solicitors' costs for the winding up of the relationship between Annie Horniman and the National Theatre Society and incorporating a new 'National Theatre Society Limited'.

Annie Horniman, the patron of the National Theatre Society since its inception, stopped her subsidy to the Society after legal wrangling which took several years. The final straw in the stormy relationship appears to be the theatre's failure to remain dark the day after the death of Edward VII.

The playwright Lennox Robinson was in charge of the Abbey Theatre that day. As both Lady Gregory and W.B. Yeats were out of the city and the response to his telegram to Lady Gregory was delayed; he let the matinée performance of *Thomas Muskerry* by Pádraic Colum go on, believing that he was adhering to the Society's policy to ignore politics.

Horniman was completely dissatisfied with the directors' handling of her objections. After protracted negotiations, she paid the last year of subsidy the Abbey would receive from her and her final telegram to the poet and director of the theatre, W.B. Yeats, marked the end of their relationship:

YOU HAVE SHOWN ME I DO NOT MATTER IN YOUR EYES THE MONEY IS PAID SUPERMEN CANNOT ASSOCIATE WITH SLAVES MAY TIME REAWAKEN YOUR SENSE OF HONOUR THEN YOU MAY FIND YOUR FRIEND AGAIN BUT REPEN-TANCE MUST COME FIRST.

ABBEY THEATRE

❖

THURSDAY, FRIDAY and SATURDAY, at 8.15.

SATURDAY MATINEE at 2.30—

THE PIE-DISH,

A Tragedy, by George Fitzmaurice.

THE ELOQUENT DEMPSEY,

A Comedy in three acts, by William Boyle.

Prices—3s, 2s, 1s, and 6d.   Booking at Cramers

King George V believed this stamp produced in
1911 made him look like 'a stuffed monkey'.
It was replaced with a traditional
side-profile stamp.

Portrait of W.B. Yeats by John Singer Sargent.

Literary Life

Dublin produced many brilliant writers in the first decades of the twentieth century. Some, including Seán O'Casey, then living in East Wall and working on the railways, published masterpieces as the century progressed. Above them all towers James Joyce. By 1911 Joyce was living in Trieste, but we owe a great deal of our knowledge of what Dublin was like at the turn of the last century to his writing. It has been said that, if Dublin were destroyed, it could be reconstructed as it was in 1904 from *Ulysses*.

Using the structure of the Homeric Odyssey, *Ulysses* records various journeys undertaken by Leopold Bloom and Stephen Dedalus across the city on an ordinary weekday: Thursday, 16 June 1904. Joyce's model for 'stately, plump Buck Mulligan', Oliver St John Gogarty, lived in Ely Place in 1911, and seems to have momentarily forgotten that ☞

This Harry Clarke drawing is a design for the book jacket of Lennox Robinson's play *Crabbed Youth and Age*. Harry Clarke attended the Dublin Metropolitan School of Art and became a well-known stained glass artist. He won a gold medal at the Board of Education National Competition in London, for his window the *Consecration of St. Mel, Bishop of Longford, by St. Patrick* in 1911.

HE CAME DOWN SPREAD LEGS ON A MULE.

From *Kiltartan wonder book* by Lady Gregory. Illustration by her daughter-in-law, Margaret Gregory.

The story of the Mule begins thus:
'Well, I will tell you the story of a Mule was in the world one time, says the old man who had promised me a codfish and had only brought me a hake. There were three sons of a King that had died, and they were living together, and there was a stable and a bird, and one of the sons was a bit simple.'

he was married when filling out his census form (he first wrote 'single', then crossed it out and wrote 'married').

If Joyce represents one pole of Ireland's remarkable early-twentieth-century literary renaissance, William Butler Yeats (listed in the census as staying in Nolan's Hotel with Augusta, Lady Gregory on South Frederick Street) represents the other. He spent a good deal of time in London, but was intensely involved in the cultural politics of Dublin at this time. A co-founder of the Abbey Theatre, he and Lady Gregory nurtured John Millington Synge, and defended him against conservative rabble-rousing when necessary. Yeats was also redefining poetry and creating a body of work which won him the Nobel Prize in 1923. It would be hard to overestimate Yeats's overwhelming effect on Irish literature and politics during this most volatile of decades.

The Abbey Theatre was founded in 1904 in collaboration with the Fay brothers, Frank and William, and funded by patrons Edward Martyn and Annie Horniman. It was a central part of the Irish Literary revival, with an emphasis on plays dealing with Irish peasant life and Irish mythology, feeding on the creation of Celtic studies as an international discipline. The Abbey opened in December 1904 with plays by Yeats and Augusta, Lady Gregory. In 1907 there was an organised nationalist disruption of J.M. Synge's *The Playboy of the Western World*.

The Gaelic revival in the last decades of the nineteenth century involved a resurgence of interest in the Irish language and ancient Irish folklore, songs and art. Although the literary life of Dublin was not dominated by the Gaelic revival, it was redefined by it. Irish language revival societies, notably Conradh na Gaeilge (the Gaelic League), founded by Douglas Hyde (Dubhglas de hÍde) fostered the teaching and use of Irish, and ultimately produced a new generation of Irish writers. The extent to which poetry and politics fused in Dublin became obvious in the years immediately after 1911, with the poet Pádraig Pearse's involvement in the rebellion at Easter 1916.

Nationalist literary societies were prominent in the city, though many were more concerned with social gathering than intellectual discourse. At the vanguard of the cultural nationalist movement was D.P. Moran, who coined the phrase 'Irish Ireland'. Moran wrote clever, scurrilous articles attacking people of all persuasions in his newspaper, *The Leader*. This was one of a range of papers in the city, including the *Irish Times*, the *Irish Independent* and the *Freeman's Journal*, all of which were aligned with one or other strand of politics.

The newspaper industry employed a large number of creative people as journalists, sub-editors and story writers. But perhaps the single most important event in 1911 for both literature and newspapers in the city was the birth, in Strabane, Co. Tyrone, of the novelist, journalist and satirist, Brian O'Nolan, better known as Flann O'Brien or Myles na gCopaleen. ✳

FREEMAN'S JOURNAL,
17 MARCH 1911

ST. PATRICK'S BALL

TO-NIGHT'S FUNCTION AT BALLSBRIDGE

Few events have canvassed with more eager anticipation that the great fancy dress ball to be held at the Royal Dublin Society's Premises, Ballsbridge, to-night, under the patronage of their Excellencies the Lord Lieutenant and the Countess of Aberdeen. There is every indication that it will be one of the most brilliant and successful functions held in Dublin for some time past. No effort has been spared by the Committee to cater for the comfort and enjoyment of all who attend, and it may safely be said that the arrangements are complete in every detail. Already some 700 tickets have been sold, but on no account will there be any overcrowding. The Hall of Industries, in which the ball will be held, is a very spacious structure, but to prevent the slightest possibility of overcrowding the number of tickets has been strictly limited. The offices (Ely House, Ely Place) will be open to-day from 12 to 4 and those who have not yet secured their tickets are advised to make early application. As already announced, special late trains will run to Dalkey, Rathmines, and Terenure and Phoenix Park, via North Circular road…

FREEMAN'S JOURNAL, 18 MARCH 1911

ST. PATRICK'S DAY

THE CELEBRATION IN DUBLIN.

Despite the rather discouraging weather conditions which marked yesterday's early forenoon, the streets of Dublin quickly assumed the animated and bustling aspect peculiar to the National Festival. The significance and inspiration of the occasion are too strong to yield to the influences of hostile climatic circumstances, and although the outlook of the opening hours of the day was by no means reassuring, there were the usual spectacles of busy streets alive with crowds of worshippers intent on fulfilling the religious obligation of the Festival, and holiday-makers bent

for the different railway ter-
mini, determined to make the
best of the day in the country.

St. Patrick's Day is now,
both in name and reality, the
national holiday, and all over
the city the indications were
such as could justify no
stranger in thinking otherwise.
There was a complete suspen-
sion of business, except in the
licensed houses, and when,
with the arrival of noon, the de-
pressing weather conditions
disappeared and the day put on
a bright and more promising
character, a responsive spirit
manifested itself in the crowd,
to whom the indoor and outdoor attractions appealed.

The only notable change in
the observance of the day in
Dublin this year has been the
abandonment of the Lord
Mayor's procession, due to the
decision of the present occu-
pant of the Mayoral Chair.

KILKENNY CASTLE

The great rush of BIRDS

On the night of March 29th, a great rush of birds was observed in several towns of S. E. Ireland, and also at some light-stations along the coast from Balbriggan to the Old Head of Kinsale…

Mr Peter Griffin of Waterford writing on March 30th, says "Last night, between ten and twelve, an extremely large number of birds was seen hovering round the city. The telegraph wires along the quay were full. Where there was any light in a window they were dashing against it… A postman when cycling across the bridge said that the birds were so numerous that he was struck by them several times. Between four and five in the morning they appeared like a cloud which covered several miles, and flew in a N.E. direction. Many remained about the city. Hundreds were found dead, especially along the quay… The streets were practically littered in the morning with the bodies of dead birds."…

Turning now to the light-stations on the coast, the most northerly from which any special number of birds was reported is Balbriggan. Mr. E. A. Kennedy, lightkeeper, at an interview, said: "A rush of Starlings commenced at eleven p.m. on March 29th, and continued until four a.m. the next morning. Fifteen were picked up dead."…

This year, for weeks previous to the 29th of that month, cold northerly or easterly winds prevailed over France and the British Isles, and birds though desirous to migrate were held back by the weather, and many species, which would otherwise have travelled separately, collected in the South of Europe like passengers at a railway station, anxious to proceed upon their journey, but unable to do so owing to a breakdown on the line…

The wind…suddenly changed to the S. at Valentia, Pembroke and the Scilly Islands on the morning of the 29th…This favourable change…liberated the birds… Unfortunately for the birds, the change took place exactly on the last day of the last quarter of the moon, the very worst night, as far as darkness is concerned, that could have happened for the birds.

The weary travellers, believing that their journey was almost concluded and baffled and bewildered by the fog or mist which probably extended twenty or thirty miles from the Irish coast, were attracted by the lighthouse lanterns and subsequently by the glare of the town lamps.

S1 S2 M3 T4 W5 ◖T6 F7 S8 S9 M10 T11 W12 ○ T13 F14 S15 S16 M17 T18 W19 T20 ◗ F21 S22 S23 M24 T25 W26 T27 ● F28 S29 S30 M31

Holidays and Observances

6…First Quarter, 5.55am   7…Old Lady Day   13…Full Moon, 2.37pm   14…Good Friday   16…Easter Sunday

17…Bank Holiday   21…Last Quarter, 6.36pm   28…New Moon, 10.25pm Total Eclipse of the Sun, invisible throughout the British Isles

CENSUS NIGHT

INSTRUCTIONS TO BE OBSERVED

Every householder in Ireland has now received a census form. He will, as he has already been made aware, have to fill it up with the required particulars...

* * *

The usefulness of the census is a matter that lies with the people themselves...The census is not an inquisition, but a work undertaken by the Government in the interests of the people themselves; for the information that is gained is often of great value in the realm of what may be called national sociology.

THE CENSUS

To-morrow night householders, hotel-keepers and all other persons charged by Act of Parliament with the duty of filling up the Census papers will attack the task. It may be that some have already prepared the return. During the past week the enumerators in Great Britain and Ireland have been engaged in the distribution of the papers. In Great Britain this work is entrusted to civilians; in this country it affords additional employment to about four thousand policemen, and no complaint has yet been made that the extra duty, which brings a small remuneration, has interfered with the ordinary discipline of the force. But it is not quite clear why this distinction should be made in the machinery of distribution and collection. That the system adopted in the case of Ireland is more economical than that of Great Britain may be granted. So excessive is the police force, and so few are its cares, that a slight addition to its responsibilities, without competition, can be imposed.

THE CENSUS

Sir – Now that everyone has sent in a census return – or has evaded doing so, or accidentally omitted it, as the case may be – I suppose we shall all fold our hands and go to sleep. We may all feel tranquilly thankful that ten years must elapse before we are called upon to fill up another – nay, some of us may reflect that in ten years we shall have gone where enumerators cease from troubling and heads of families are at rest. Still, it is open to the enquiring mind to ask what it has all been for...

2 April 1911 CENSUS Day

In the weeks before census day, Sunday 2 April, more than 4,000 census enumerators across Ireland distributed the large blue census forms to every home. As they moved from house to house the enumerators listed every head of household, before leaving behind the form to be filled in. Unlike in Britain, where a special civilian staff was recruited for the job, the enumerators in Ireland were drawn from the ranks of the RIC. In Dublin, the constabulary was supplemented by 160 members of the Dublin Metropolitan Police.

This was an entirely sensible move according to the local press in Dublin, which argued that the police were under-employed and that they had expert knowledge of localities and personalities, as well as the experience of filing reports, to help them to carry out their task in the correct manner. Filling out the form correctly was deemed in newspaper editorials to be a task which 'leaves little room for mistake by a person of ordinary intelligence.' Nonetheless, this census included a more

detailed list of questions than in previous censuses, inspiring what the *Freeman's Journal* called 'professional humourists' to make fun of the difficulties presented.

The census form for Ireland was different from that distributed in Britain. On the Irish form there was a question asking the religion of every person in a household. This question was not included in the British form. On the Irish form there was a question seeking to ascertain the number of Irish speakers in the country. In Britain, that question was asked of Welsh speakers. Finally, in Ireland the question was posed as to whether people could: 'Read and Write', 'Read Only', or 'Cannot Read'. Such a question was not asked in Britain and, as one Irish newspaper noted, 'why it should be so is not easy to understand'.

Collection of the census was to begin on Monday 3 April, and all forms were to be forwarded eventually to Charlemont House on

Rutland Square where the Census Commissioners for Ireland (led by Sir William Thompson, the registrar general, and Edward O'Farrell, assistant under-secretary) had established a system for dealing with them. Almost 200 specialist workers, including 100 boy assistants, were engaged in the work of tabulation.

Sunday 2 April 1911 passed off in much the same way as any other Sunday in Dublin, defined by the formal demands of religious observance. Dublin was a quiet place on a Sunday; the shops and the-atres were closed, and few events took place. There was, for example, an exhibition at the Royal Hibernian Academy on Lower Abbey Street, which required an entrance fee of 1 shilling.

A number of preachers were speaking in Dublin on that day. Rev. Thomas O'Brien had come from Cork to preach a special sermon to appeal for donations from the Catholics of Dublin for St Mary's Training School in Stanhope Street. That institution had been founded in 1811, and 100 years later was home to 113 young girls, many of whom had been orphaned. In the course of the sermon, Fr O'Brien outlined how the nuns of Stanhope Street trained the girls in laundry and sewing before securing positions in wider society for them once they came of age.

Also preaching in the city on that day was the Jesuit Fr Robert Kane, who was into the fifth of his extended series of Lenten lectures. Fr Kane drew a huge crowd to St Francis Xavier's church on Upper Gardiner Street to hear him preach about the

'Sores of Society'. For their part the Protestant churches of Dublin were holding an appeal to raise money for the Board of Religious Education, which organised daily and weekly instruction in religion for children across the city.

Sport offered a limited escape to Dubliners, but even this was curtailed by religion. Traditions of sabbatarianism meant that rugby, soccer, horse racing, golf and other sporting events had been played on Saturday as was usual. That weekend there had been an international match of sorts in the city when the British Army in Ireland XI played the British Army in England XI in a soccer match at Dalymount Park. Saturday had also seen a full round of rugby club matches and local golf tournaments.

On Sunday evening, the Grocers' Assistants' Society was staging the third round of its billiards competition but, by and large, this and every other Sunday was a day when the Gaelic Athletic Association dominated the sporting life of the city. The usual round of hurling and football league matches were played in grounds all across Dublin. The highlight, however, was the Dublin county championship matches played at the new ground on Jones's Road (renamed Croke Park in 1913).

The centre spectacle was the senior football match between the Kickhams club and the O'Connells of Kingstown. Also played was the fraught local junior hurling derby match between two clubs who came in from the villages of Lusk and Naul in north Dublin. Naul won a narrow, low-scoring match which was judiciously described as 'competitive'. The third match to be played was a junior football contest between the Hibernian Knights and Thomas Davis from Tallaght. It was a triple bill which drew a fine crowd.

As the footballers of Thomas Davis were taking the field in Croke Park, the name of the old Young Irelander was being evoked across the city in Blackrock. The members of the Thomas Davis players, a sub-group of the local Thomas Davis Society, were meeting in Blackrock People's Park to practice for a play they intended to put on later in the month. In conjunction with the Gaelic League, the Davis Players were scheduled to perform *O'Donnell's Cross* by L. MacManus at the Town Hall in Blackrock at the end of April.

On 1 April, Miss Evie Green was the headline act at the Theatre Royal on Hawkins Street, and Frank Lister was playing twice nightly at the Tivoli on Francis Street. ❋

SUFFRAGISTS
AND THE CENSUS

Female suffragists had been active in Ireland since the 1870s, in organisations that were run by figures like Anna Haslam and which did not engage in militant action. But in November 1908 Hanna Sheehy Skeffington and Margaret Cousins, along with their feminist husbands, Francis Sheehy Skeffington and James Cousins, founded the Irish Women's Franchise League (IWFL). In November 1910, six IWFL members, including Margaret Cousins, were imprisoned in London when they participated in protests organised by the Women's Social and Political Union (WSPU). They broke the windows in the chief secretary for Ireland, Augustine Birrell's London home by throwing potatoes through them and were later arrested for similar escapades on Downing Street.

Soon after this, the census of 1911 provided an occasion to suffragists to demonstrate their discontent. As James Cousins put it, 'the census was a prime opportunity of throwing metaphorical spanners in official machinery'. As with suffrage militancy in general, a boycott of the census was not an idea indigenous to Ireland. The proposal to boycott the census emerged in Britain where, as in Ireland, the census was fixed for 2 April. This campaign was led by the WSPU and another militant organisation, the Women's Freedom League, operating under the slogan 'No Vote, No Census'. These groups announced that as women were not treated as full citizens though were required to pay taxes, their members would not fill out the census form as required by law.

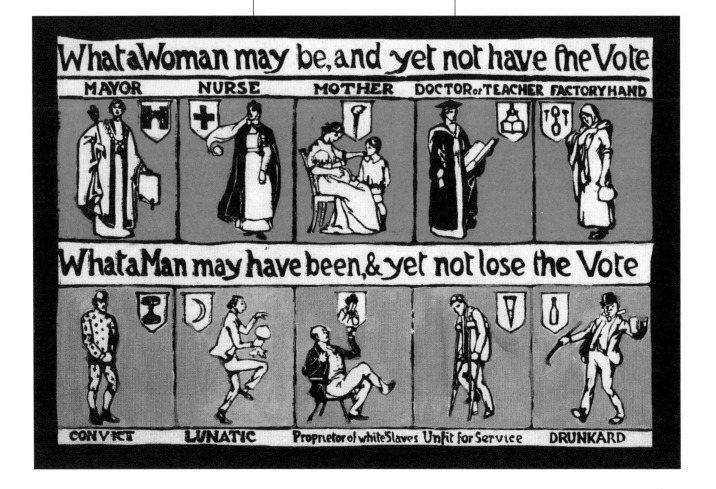

From March 1911 onwards there was voluminous correspondence in the *Irish Times* and *Freeman's Journal* on the proposed boycott. Most moderate feminists were opposed to the boycott, seeing the census as an essential planning tool, and refusal to engage with it as wrong-headed and counter-productive.

On the Saturday night of 1 April, the committee of the IWFL was holding a meeting in the Antient Concert Rooms in Dublin, when a policeman entered and inquired if the women intended to hold a meeting again the following evening. He was told that there was no such intention, but that they had requisitioned a number of aeroplanes and submarines, the better to avoid filling out the census. It was illegal to refuse to fill out the census form, and could only be avoided if one was not in the country.

So what happened on 2 April? Notably there were no public gatherings or protests in Ireland. It is not clear why the Irish census evaders decided against public demonstrations. The most likely reason is that they would not have been able to muster large numbers. As already pointed out, Irish suffragism was in a period of transition; suffragist militancy in the country was as yet in its infancy with only a small cohort of militant activists.

Further, the organisers of the protest almost certainly hoped that a less demonstrative approach would facilitate the participation of moderates in the census evasion. Indeed, a suffragette correspondent to the *Freeman's Journal* wrote that 'Several of our friends have recently congratulated us on the constitutional and eminently ladylike nature of census resistance. In fact it is on that very account being very widely adopted in Ireland'. Getting about in town at night without male chaperones was not considered ladylike, and in any case, Dublin in 1911 did not offer the range of public spaces that London suffragists, who were organising large protests, had available to them, especially not at night.

The digitised 1911 census reveals firm evidence of the evasion attempts of several women. Heads of households were responsible for filling out the form, and women who were heads of households and did not make the return invited prosecution. A boycotting woman who was not the head of household placed her relative in danger of prosecution. It seems that the leadership of the IWFL, in an effort to avoid this second eventuality, gathered at least some boycotters in small groups in houses which for various reasons were not enumerated. This tactic was also adopted in Britain (see the photograph from Britain, with 'No Vote, No Census' sign inside the house and women gathered together to sleep on census night).

James Cousins and Francis Sheehy Skeffington attempted to keep their wives' names out of the census forms, but were defeated by the police enumerators, who reinstated them. Many women used the 'Infirmity' section of the form (which specified deaf, dumb, blind, idiot, imbecile ☞

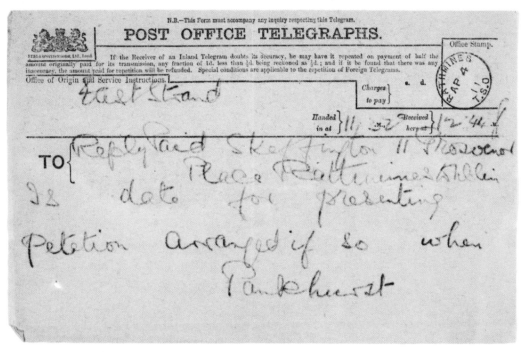

POST OFFICE TELEGRAPHS.

Left: Telegram to Hanna Sheehy Skeffington from the leader of the British suffragette movement, Emmeline Pankhurst, dated April 4, 1911: 'Is date for presenting petition arranged if so when Pankhurst'.

Below left: Postcard showing women sleeping on floor on census night in a building that was not registered for a census return, poster saying: 'No Vote, No Census'

Right: 'Handicapped!': Propaganda poster for the Artists' Suffrage League shows a woman in a rowboat, struggling in high waves, while a man relaxes on a sailboat with a sail labelled 'votes'. Westminster Palace can be seen in the background.

HANDICAPPED!

CARL HENTSCHEL LTD 182, 183 & 184 FLEET ST E.C.   PUBLISHED BY THE ARTISTS' SUFFRAGE LEAGUE

THE SUFFRAGETTE THAT KNEW JIU-JITSU. THE ARREST.

Cartoon in Punch *depicting the phenomenon of Edith Garrud. She was a suffragette, who trained other women in jiu-jitsu so that they could protect the leaders of the suffragette movement against arrest.*

☞ or lunatic as possible entries) to register their discontent by writing 'voteless' or 'unenfranchised'. Tom Kettle, husband of Mary Kettle, sister to Hanna Sheehy Skeffington, signed the form with the annotation 'Signature of one of the Heads of the Family'.

It seems clear that the numbers who succeeded in evading enumeration in Ireland were small indeed, but that supporters of female suffragism in Ireland utilised the census to protest in a variety of ways beyond the simplest and most extreme form of

protest, the boycott. The protest emphasised the divisions within Irish suffragism rather than uniting them, but it marked a further stage on the road to full-scale militant activity in Ireland. ❀

SPEED OF MOTORS

THE PROPOSED LIMIT IN DUBLIN

INTERESTING INTERVIEWS

A representative of the "Irish Independent" interviewed various people in Dublin yesterday to ascertain their opinion of the proposal to limit the speed of motor cars in the city.

With reference to this question the Local Government Board will hold an inquiry at the City Hall on Monday next in accordance with an application made at the meeting of the Dublin Corporation on the 13th March that "in view of the many accidents arising from reckless motor driving in the city this Council (Municipal) request the L.G. Board for Ireland to fix the rate of speed for motors at the same limit as that prescribed for horse traffic within the city boundary."

"Even for Dublin Corporation," said a prominent official connected with the motor car trade, "such a resolution is an absurd anomaly. First, because there is no fixed speed limit for 'horse traffic' in the city, and secondly, because there has not been a single instance within the past 12 months of a motorist being fined for, or charged with 'reckless driving' within the city boundary.

"There is a speed limit in the Park of 20 miles an hour, and in the city a limit of 10 miles for vans, which would probably include motor vans. The great object of legislation naturally is to safeguard the public, and the law is regarding vehicular traffic is already sufficiently comprehensive.

"Many people are not aware that the Dublin hackney cars are compelled (by the Dublin Police Carriage Fares Bye-laws Act, 1905) to drive at least at a rate of six miles an hour, unless the fare requests them to go slower, but there is no limit as to what higher speeds they may travel – except the limitation of the horse or the inclination of the driver. The great advantage of the three 'don'ts' imposed on horse and motor drivers alike – don't endanger yourself or the public, or drive without proper control of the horse or vehicle – applies to all parts of the city and makes a speed limit unnecessary. A motor car going 30 miles an hour on a clear stretch of road in the Park, or 15 miles an hour in parts of O'Connell street, is less dangerous than a motor or hackney car going six miles an hour at North Earl street or Grafton street corners.

COMPARISON OF CASUALTIES

"The best answer to the reckless charge of 'reckless driving' is the list of the street accidents in Dublin during the year 1910, as furnished by the Home Office. In considering this it must also be remembered that each motor vehicle covers, at least, about three times as much mileage in a year as a horse-drawn vehicle; that is relatively the accidents should be three times more numerous for motors allowing the same individual standard of care and efficiency in both classes of drivers. For the year 1910 there were 1,379 motor cars and 1,381 motor cycles in use in the Dublin metropolitan area, or a total of 2,760 motor vehicles. Hackney cars numbered 852, and cabs 633 – a total of 1,485 horse-drawn vehicles.

Another gentleman interested in the motor car business pointed out that there are upwards of 1,180 police in Dublin, or more than double the proportion according to population, of the London force. If these are armed with stop-watches to check the speeds of motor cars in the city, he said, motoring in Dublin will be regular nightmare.

He thought the ridiculousness of the proposal would be shown if all motor cars in Dublin at present were to proceed at less than six miles an hour on any one day in Dublin. The whole traffic would be completely blocked, he predicted, and people would soon ask them to "move on" out of the way. The present vehicular traffic in the streets should be better regulated, and each vehicle kept to the proper side of the thoroughfare, especially in going round corners.

THE DOCTOR DILEMMA

Discussing the proposal to limit motor cars to the indefinite speed prescribed by the Corporation ☞

	Vehicles	Fatal Accidents	Non-fatal
HORSE	1485	7	219
MOTOR	2,760	7	77

'Speed Limit' cartoon from the *Sunday Independent*.

resolution, a well-known Dublin physician said any restriction on the speed of motor cars would seriously affect medical men who use such cars. In the first place, he said, doctors are ordinary citizens and ratepayers as well as the most solicitous members of the Corporation and are at least as keenly interested in the safety of public traffic as anyone else.

They did not, he said, use cars, as a rule, for pleasure, and there was a reason for so many of them adopting the modern convenience afforded by the motor car, and that is its safety, its speed, and its utility at all hours of the day or night. He estimated that about eighty doctors in Dublin possessed motor cars, and had invested in them at an average £500 a car, a total of about £40,000. If the speed were reduced to the hackney car level, all this money would be a dead loss pratically. He instanced a case in which he was engaged recently. A patient lay dying from suffocation, and a critical operation had to be performed as soon as possible. In his motor he reached the house at least twenty minutes before he could have done so by a cab or hackney car, and those minutes' delay would have meant the death of the patient.

PEDESTRIAN POINT OF VIEW

Several ordinary "men in the street" were also queried on the subject. They were all non-motorists, and had not the slightest partiality for a motorist as a motorist or for an owner of any other class of vehicle as such, but they were all unanimous in one opinion – that the proposed restriction was not required in Dublin.

In a few words, their views may be summed up in the remark made by an old Dublin clergyman, who said, "there is no necessity for any restriction of the kind, as Dublin motorists, as far as I have experience of them, are careful and considerate. Strangers, especially in Horse Show Week, and some foreign trippers are the chief offenders in endangering the public by motor dashing through the streets. The legal restrictions at present in force are quite sufficient for our Dublin motorists."

It may be added that the only places in Ireland – or except a few particular streets in London, and some other cities in Great Britain – where speed limits are imposed on motorists are Bray (8 miles an hour), Bangor (6 miles an hour in certain streets), and Carrickfergus (10 miles an hour). But the Bray bye-law, we are informed, has never been sanctioned by the L.G.B.

COLLAPSE
OF
TENEMENT
HOUSES IN
DUBLIN

TWO WORKMEN INJURED

Three derelict tenement houses in Church street collapsed yesterday, the occurrence resulting in injuries to two men who were at work razing the dilapidated fabric. The premises in question were 146, 148, and 150 May lane, Church street. The accident occurred about half-past four.

The men injured were two of a number in the employment of Mr. Thomas Doherty, contractor, who were engaged in the work referred. Their names are Patrick Hussell, of Church street, and Harry Bambreke, of 1 Henrietta place. The former was able to walk to hospital, where his injuries were dressed. Bambreke was more seriously injured. He was overwhelmed by the debris, and both his legs were broken. He was conveyed in the city ambulance to the Richmond Hospital, where one of his legs was amputated.

FREEMAN'S JOURNAL,
12 APRIL 1911

THE HOUSING PROBLEM IN DUBLIN

A proposal to appoint a Committee to deal solely with the housing question will soon be submitted to the Corporation. It is based on the necessity for concentrated and sustained effort in this direction, and responds to the desire so insistently expressed in many quarters that the problem of the slum should be attached with increased energy in the interest of the physical and moral health of the poorer population. The Housing Committee would devote itself to the utilisation of the powers possessed by the Corporation, and would also consider how private enterprise could be encouraged. Help from any quarter in dealing with the evil should be welcomed. It is sufficiently evident that the task cannot be accomplished by the Corporation as promptly as reformers desire. The question of ways and means obtrudes itself at once; and the experience of the municipal body in housing schemes shows that that question is of greater importance in Dublin than it would be in many another city of similar size. The site of a house in Bride street which had a frontage of twenty-two feet cost the Corporation £7,000. This fact, mentioned by the Lord Mayor at the meeting yesterday of the Sick and Indigent Roomkeepers' Society, illustrates one of the difficulties which the Corporation has had to encounter in its attempt to clear the slums and to provide for the working classes dwelling fit for human habitation. The experience of the Council has been disappointing enough to paralyse effort; yet several new schemes have been undertaken, and it is hoped that they will be self-supporting.

Harsh criticism of the efforts of the Corporation cannot be well-informed. No tendency of this kind manifested itself at the meeting of the Sick and Indigent Roomkeepers' Society, which works among the poor and knows what has been done for them and what remains to be done. By more than one speaker the opinion was expressed that the Corporation had accomplished excellent work; and it was fitting that Father Monahan should, in this connection, pay a tribute to the princely philanthropy of Lord Iveagh. The dividend to the Corporation and the private benefactor has come in the shape of a marked improvement in the public health. Twenty years ago the death rate of the city was 38 per thousand; last year it was 19. The enforcement of sanitary laws by the Public Health Department has conduced largely to this result, but one of the most effective factors was the demolition of foul rookeries, to be replaced by clean and decent dwellings. As the work progresses, the good effects will be felt not only by the classes to be directly benefited, but by the whole community. The evil influence of the typical slum is to be witnessed in cases which come under the notice of magistrates and judges as well as in cases of which the sanitary inspector and the doctor have to take account. Those who look for more temperate habits among the people, and a diminution of crime of every sort, base their hopes on improved housing conditions.

The subject was one of the many, bearing on the lives of the poor, which were discussed by the friends and supporters of the Roomkeepers' Society at their annual meeting. The one hundredth and twentieth year of this charity finds it capable of rendering splendid service to the suffering poor. Last year more than eight thousand families, representing almost thirty-two thousand persons, were relieved when they most needed help. Honest, decent folk were enabled to tide over their difficulties and to stand up again in the struggle for a living. But the claims are many, despite the other charitable agencies at work in the city.

DEATH
OF AN
INJURED
WATCHMAN

Henry Bambreke, the watchman who was injured by the falling debris of tenement houses in May lane, on Monday afternoon, died yesterday morning, in the Richmond Hospital, from his injuries. An inquest will be held to-day.

Aylward's Yard, rear of Thomas Street.

In 1911 Dublin had the worst housing conditions of any city in the United Kingdom (Glasgow came a close second). 26,000 families lived in inner-city tenements, and 20,000 of these families lived in single-room dwellings. These families sometimes comprised three generations, and occasionally, as in the census return for the Dixon family in Buckingham Street, non-family members; the Dixons had a nurse-child (foster-child), Thomas Power, living with them. In Mabbot Street and Tyrone Street, seventeen families kept lodgers, most in spite of living in just one room. Our modern ideas of privacy are severely challenged by the difficulties implicit in single-room, multi-generational occupancy. ☞

POVERTY

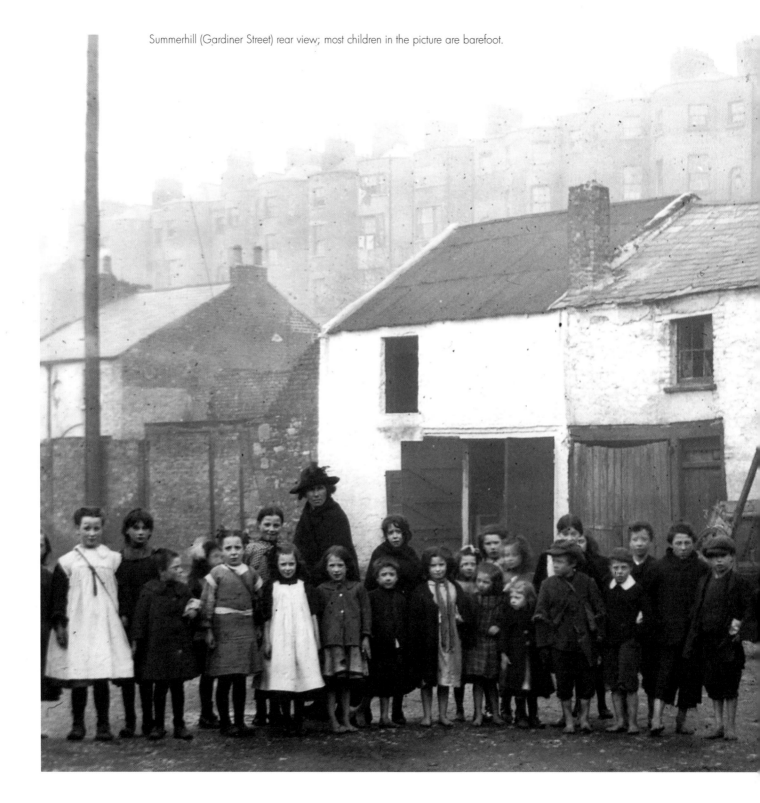

Summerhill (Gardiner Street) rear view; most children in the picture are barefoot.

☞ Henrietta Street, which had once been home to bishops, peers and members of parliament, exemplifies the chronic overcrowding in the tenements at this period. An astonishing 835 people lived in fifteen houses. There were members of nineteen different families living in No. 7. Among the 104 people who shared the house were charwomen, domestic servants, labourers, porters, messengers, painters, carpenters, pensioners, a postman, a tailor, and a whole class of school children.

Tenement dwellers died younger, more often from tuberculosis, and more often in childhood; see the very high child mortality (six survivors from thirteen children) in the Dixon household. Some died as the buildings they lived in collapsed around them. Tenements owned by Mrs Ryan on Church Street, for example, collapsed in 1913, killing up to seven people. Overall, the death rate in Dublin per thousand was 22.3; in London it was just 15.6.

This was not helped by the unsanitary conditions of inner-city tenements, where livestock was kept in dairy yards, cattle yards and down side lanes. Drainage was little better than rudimentary, and most of the meat eaten in the city came from beasts slaughtered in small private abattoirs and slaughter-houses. Offal and animal excrement lay on city streets despite this being forbidden in a series of acts, such as the Nuisance Acts, through the nineteenth century.

People living in tenements were failed by Dublin Corporation, the city authority, which did not develop a meaningful policy to improve tenement life. A Housing Inquiry in 1914 found that sixteen members of the Corporation owned tenements, and it was clear that Corporation members had been intervening to foil the enforcement of regulations against their properties. The Corporation did successfully carry out a number of social housing projects, including building Benburb Street and Corporation Buildings off the north quays. Other initiatives from the Dublin Artisans' Dwelling Company and the Iveagh Trust provided greatly improved housing for the working class, but were necessarily limited in scale.

Many families were forced to send their children out on the street selling wares. A 1902 report dealing with the problem of the thousands of street-selling children noted that in one in six cases, one or both parents were dead. Others were from homes affected by illness, drunkenness or unemployment. Help for some destitute children came from Mrs Smyly's Homes and Schools, eleven of which were based in the city. The Coombe Ragged School was run for young Protestant boys, and the Dublin Working Boys Home and Harding Technical School operated on Lord Edward Street and was intended for boys working in the city who did not live with their parents.

Many children also ended up in confinement. There were several penitentiaries for children across the city, including High Park Reformatory for Girls, most of whom were committed for petty theft. Boys could also be sent to prison or to industrial ☞

McGinnis's Court, off Townsend Street. Boy with injured foot.

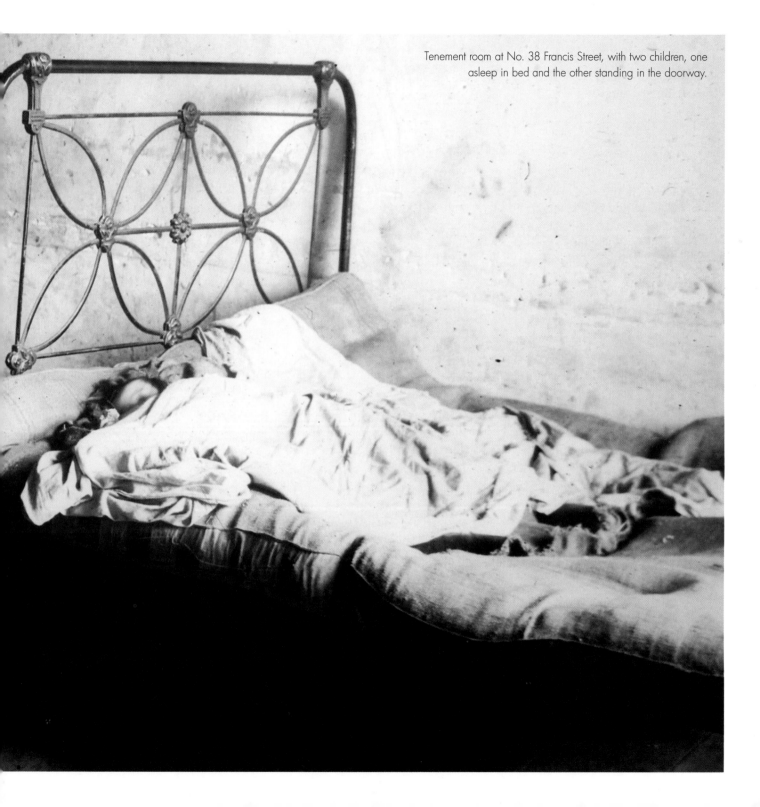

Tenement room at No. 38 Francis Street, with two children, one asleep in bed and the other standing in the doorway.

schools such as the now notorious Artane.

Many women tried to make money as street dealers, selling fish, flowers, old clothes, pigs, fruit and much more. Some worked at home making various items such as bags, hats, vests and dresses, and some worked in laundries and restaurants. Large numbers of women worked as domestic servants; even lower-middle-class families had servants, who would get room and board and a small wage if they were lucky. Some were forced to turn to prostitution on the streets or in brothels, often ending up in Mountjoy Prison.

For those living in poverty, some succour came from the Liberal government of Herbert Asquith and David Lloyd George, arguably the most radical administration to govern Ireland in the twentieth century. Its legacy included the introduction of old-age pensions in 1908, labour exchanges in 1909, and a national insurance scheme in 1911 to afford workers protection against sickness, invalidity and unemployment. The introduction of the old-age pension for the over-70s was of enormous importance, alleviating some of the distress that attended the last years of those no longer able to work, even if work could be found. The Liberals progressively tackled social issues, sometimes to the discomfort of the Irish Parliamentary Party, who initially voted against Lloyd George's famous 'People's Budget' in response to Irish unrest at the additional alcohol duties it imposed.

Further official relief for the poor came through the Poor Law, whereby workhouses were supposed to deal with social problems from destitution to old age, illness and abandonment. They accommodated people who were in need of short-term relief from homelessness, but they also housed those who were permanently destitute. Families were generally separated by gender into different wards on entry and were required to work around the house or the grounds. Dublin had two workhouses in 1911: the South Dublin Union on James's Street, and the North Dublin Union on North Brunswick Street. Workhouses were also the inappropriate homes for many who suffered from long-term mental illness, becoming de facto asylums. More dedicated treatment for mental illness was provided in institutions such as the Central Mental Hospital and the Richmond Asylum.

Charities attempted to fill the gaps left by the state. For example, the Sick and Indigent Roomkeepers' Society, founded in Dublin in 1790, offered assistance without religious or moral pressures, from its house at Palace Street. Mostly, though, people struggled to survive through their own informal networks: the unemployed, the elderly and the infirm, as well as those who had lost spouses or parents, were supported by the able. This was as true for the labourers of the Dublin countryside as it was for those of the city.

Dublin supported many pawnshops offering immediate relief to

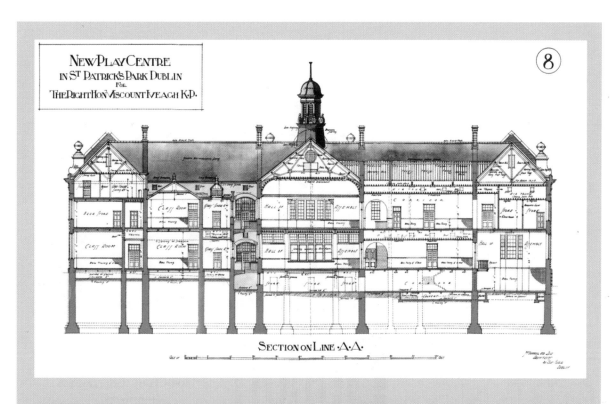

NEW PLAY CENTRE
IN ST PATRICK'S PARK DUBLIN
FOR
THE RIGHT HON VISCOUNT IVEAGH K·P·

⑧

SECTION ON LINE ·A·A·

The Iveagh Play Centre was commissioned by Lord Iveagh, Edward Cecil Guinness. The Play Centre was equipped with classrooms, large halls, offices and reception rooms. The Centre was to open five evenings and one morning, catering for boys and girls between the ages of three and fourteen. The children were taught a wide range of practical subjects including basket-making, mat weaving, needlework, drawing and painting, dancing, singing and gymnastics. Free refreshment, the traditional cocoa and bun, was provided to all children and mainly for this reason the Centre became known among residents of the surrounding Liberties as the 'Bay-no' (beano or party).

those in distress. Interest was high, however, and it was not unknown for people to have to pawn their essential clothing, boots and work tools, so worsening the cycle of poverty. Hundreds begged on many of Dublin's more prosperous streets, including Merrion Row and St Stephen's Green. Many were Dubliners; many more had tramped to the city, from rural areas stricken by famine or depression. ✳

IRISH TIMES,
15 APRIL 1911

THE GRAFTON PICTURE HOUSE,

72 GRAFTON STREET

OPENS

Easter Monday

Continuous performance, 12–10.30 daily. Admission, one shilling; children, sixpence; including admission to the Wedgewood and Oak rooms.

SOCIAL LIFE

In 1911 Dublin Castle was the focus of government social life, with its traditional mixture of pomp and pageantry. The lavish Castle balls and dinners were the ultimate expression of high society at play. The banquet halls were filled with guests dressed in finely ornamented clothes and splendid uniforms, and waited on by staff attired in state livery. It was a scene played out all over the British Empire. ☛

Merry's
FINEST OLD MARSALA
18

FINEST OLD
DUBLIN WHISKEY,
20/- Per Gallon.
FULLY MATURED IN SHERRY CASKS

"BASS"
In Bottle

Pub interior. Photographs of pub interiors are
difficult to find even though drinking comprised
a large element of Dublin social life.

Representing a different world were the pubs of Dublin. These were the single most notable feature of the city's social life, vibrant gathering places for all classes and in all areas. As an institution, the pub was the preserve of men, with women generally excluded. As early as 1610 a writer remarked that 'in Dublin the whole profit of the towne stands upon alehouses… there are whole streets of taverns.' Workingmen's pubs were everywhere in the city; tough, raw establishments at once providing an escape from poverty and increasing it.

In 1911 Dublin's pubs, many of them owned by country people, were thriving despite the condemnations of temperance reformers (including Matt Talbot, who lived at Rutland Street), and were the focal point of popular culture in the city. Temperance reformers sought to establish recreational facilities of their own, and they succeeded, but never to the point of threatening to displace the public house in importance.

As if to confirm this, alcohol was a frequent theme in Irish literature. Stephen Dedalus remarks in *Ulysses* how it would present a formidable challenge to cross Dublin without going past a single public house. One of the pubs which James Joyce himself was unable to pass was Davy Byrne's pub on Duke Street, which is mentioned in both *Dubliners* and *Ulysses*. In 1911 Davy Byrne himself was into his third of five decades as proprietor, while on nearby South Anne Street, John Kehoe ran a pub of great repute. Both pubs still thrive today.

Public houses were at the heart of the revival of traditional music in the city. Among the many native musicians was the piper prodigy, Leo Rowsome, then aged eight. Eamonn Ceannt, later a leader in the 1916 Rising, was also a prominent piper. Dublin was the home of several music publishers, like Pigott & Company, while there were regular concerts given at the many concert halls and band rooms, such as the Antient Concert Rooms (Joyce, who had a fine singing voice, sang there, as did Count John McCormack), and operatic performances at theatres on Burgh Quay and Hawkins Street. Living in the city

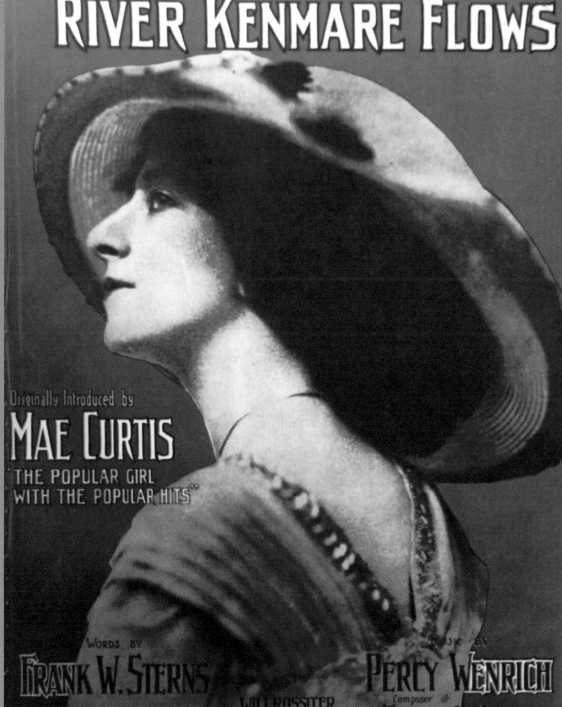

Cover of sheet music composed by Percy Wenrich, published in Chicago in 1911. The chorus reads: 'In old Ireland/Where the River Kenmare flows/In fair Erin/Where the dear old shamrock grows/there my Kathleen Mavourneen is waiting for me/In old Ireland/where the River Kenmare flows.'

QUEEN'S THEATRE.

GIGANTIC SUCCESS.

TO-NIGHT at 8. MATINEES WEDNESDAY and SATURDAY, at 2.

MESSRS. CULLEN and CARTHY'S
GRAND XMAS PANTOMIME,

"LITTLE RED RIDING HOOD."

Prices—6d. to 2s. 6d. Booking at Cramer's and Theatre. Tel. 3015. Children Half-price to all parts of house. Early Doors at 1 and 6.30.

ROUND ROOM, ROTUNDA.

IMPORTANT NOTICE !!!

OWING TO THE ENORMOUS SUCCESS AND INCREASING POPULARITY,

CARTER'S SUPERB ENTERTAINMENT
WILL BE CONTINUED FOR ONE WEEK LONGER

TWICE DAILY AT 3 AND 8 P.M.

Doors open 2.30 and 7.30. Carriages 5 and 10.15.

CARTER, CARTER,

The Mysterious.   The Talk of Dublin.

☞ were music teachers, organ builders, piano tuners, orchestral members and many other professional musicians.

The city's clubs were clear in their class divisions. As well as the workingmen's clubs, the fashionable clubs of London were replicated in Dublin. There were clubs on St Stephen's Green and on Clare Street, but the most prestigious was the Kildare Street Club, which, on census night, had 32 servants under the direction of the club steward, all to look after six visitors. Among the six visitors were a land owner, a land agent, a retired colonel, the official starter at Irish race meetings and Lord Fermoy.

Around the clubs grew up a necklace of establishments, including Prost's hairdresser and perfumer on St Stephen's Green, and Sloane's Turkish baths at Leinster Street, which Leopold Bloom visits in *Ulysses*. It was to the people who frequented the clubs that the city's antiques and fine arts dealers, like Persse's on Kildare Street,

and Young's at South Anne Street, looked for business. Dublin was home to artists like Dora Philips, landscape painters like Joseph Kavanagh, and picture framers like Richard Persse at Clarendon Street.

In 1911 the circus was in its heyday. British and continental circuses regularly visited Dublin, as there were a number of local circuses, including Duffy's and Fossett's, which was then known as Powell and Clarke's circus, and was run by a ventriloquist, Frank Lowe. Cinema had arrived in Dublin in April 1896 when a demonstration was held in Dan Lowry's Star of Erin theatre (later the Olympia). James Joyce was briefly the manager of the first cinema in the country, the Volta Electric Theatre, which opened in December 1909. This sparked the establishment of several other institutions which showed motion pictures. The first film made in Ireland was, fittingly, a tale of emigration made in 1910, called *The Lad from Old Ireland.*

Comedy and pantomime were hugely popular. Variety shows usually consisted of robust performances and bawdy sketches by troupes who often engaged with the audience. Many performers came to Ireland from England, bringing their music hall acts. The most famous venues in the city for variety and pantomime were the Theatre Royal on Hawkins Street, and the Queen's Royal Theatre on Brunswick (now Pearse) Street.

Besides popular culture, there was a range of institutions which catered for educational recreation. In 1911 the National Gallery was expanding under the direction of Walter Armstrong, and continued to do so under his successor, Hugh Lane. The National Museum's collection had been expanded through amalgamation with the Natural History Museum, and by the addition of collections from the Royal Dublin Society and the Royal Irish Academy.

The Public Libraries Act of 1902 facilitated the development of smaller libraries like the Carnegie Free Libraries across the city, while the National Library on Kildare Street and Marsh's Library on St Patrick's Close were also important institutions.

For those who preferred their relaxation outdoors, Dublin was served by a range of impressive parks, including St Stephen's Green and the People's Park in Blackrock. Pride of place was held by the Phoenix Park, stocked with deer and pheasants, and dotted with impressive houses and monuments, including the vice-regal lodge and the Wellington monument. The park had an expanse of gardens, bandstands and playing fields, and its fine zoo which has now been open since 1831.

The National Botanic Gardens in Glasnevin were renowned as a centre of horticultural excellence, filled with thousands of flowers, plants and trees. In 1911, curator Frederick Moore, who served in the position for 42 years, was knighted for work which had seen his gardens gain a reputation equal to those of Kew in London. Also, in 1911, Herbert Park was opened in Ballsbridge. Previously the site of the Irish International Exhibition in 1907, the land had been donated to the public by the Earl of Pembroke on the occasion of the coming of age of his son, Lord Herbert. ❀

ORCHIDS AT THE BOTANIC GARDENS

During his years as curator of the National Botanic Gardens, Sir Frederick Moore built the orchid collection at Glasnevin into a world leader. At the time of his death, the collection comprised more than a thousand species and over 600 hybrids. Not only did Frederick Moore purchase large numbers of plants from the firms of O'Brien, Bull, Low, Sanders, Stevens, and Veitch, but was also donated material by these same firms. Knowing Frederick Moore's fondness for the small and unusual (plants often spurned by the collectors of flamboyance and gaudiness), many firms would send him miscellaneous collections of unsold material at the end of each season. A consequence of this method of acquiring material meant that many plants were unnamed, and when these were sent to Kew for identification by Robert Rolfe, some proved to be new to science. Thus the Orchid House was the source of many new species described between the 1880s and 1920s.

Frederick Moore arranged for many of these orchids to be painted when they flowered. The Botanic Gardens still holds this collection, two from which are seen here (left and right respectively). Nearly 1,300 orchid portraits were painted by Lydia Shackleton and subsequently by Alice Jacob. Jacob portrayed several aspects of the flower to facilitate scientific study of the collection.

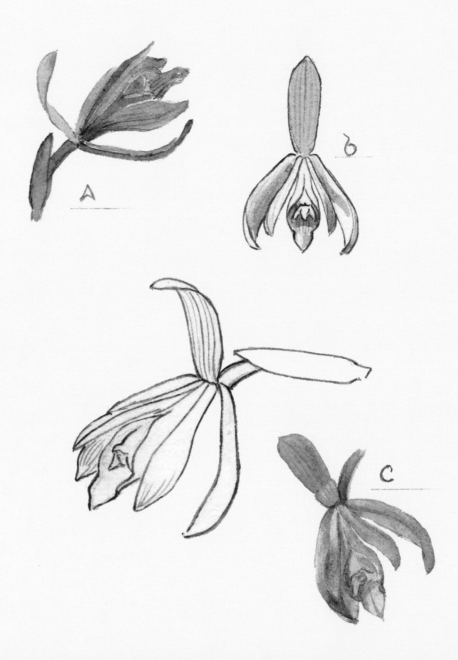

M1 T2 W3 T4 ◖F5 S6 S7 M8 T9 W10 T11 F12 ○ S13 S14 M15 T16 W17 T18 F19 S20 ◗ S21 M22 T23 W24 T25 F26 S27 ● S28 M29 T30 W31

Holidays and Observances

5…First Quarter, 1.14pm   9…Half-Quarter Day   13…Full Moon, 6.10am, Penumbral Eclipse of the Moon   14…Old May Day

21…Last Quarter, 9.23am   25…Ascension Day   28…New Moon, 6.24am

WHITE STAR LINE

Royal & United States Mail Steamers.

"OLYMPIC" & "TITANIC"
45,000 TONS EACH
The Largest Vessels in the World.

May 1911

This illustration shows the cover of a White Star Line promotional booklet, published in May 1911, which promotes the company's new super-liners, Olympic and Titanic.

WORLD'S LARGEST ANCHOR

BELFAST AND THE NORTH

BELFAST OFFICE,
108 ROYAL AVENUE.
(FROM OUR CORRESPONDENT)

The massive anchor which has been made for the White Star liner as Titanic, at present being built by Messrs. Harland and Wolff, arrived at the Belfast dock this morning. It was conveyed from Fleetwood by the Lancashire and Yorkshire and London and North-Western Railway Company's Royal Mail steamer Duke of Albany, and was discharged by means of a 25-ton crane. The anchor, which is a marvellous piece of workmanship and takes twenty horses to pull, is in weight 15 tons 16 cwt.; its width is ten feet across the head with a shank sixteen feet long. It was manufactured by Messrs. Hingley and Sons, Ltd., of Netherton Iron Works, Dubley, and at the test it withstood a strain of 117 tons. The iron in the cable supporting the anchor is 3 3/8 inches thick and the whole outfit weighs 100 tons. In addition to carrying this great anchor the Titanic will have two smaller ones weighing about eight tons each.

Launch
OF
White Star Royal Mail Triple-Screw Steamer
"TITANIC"
At BELFAST,
Wednesday, 31st May, 1911, at 12-15 p.m.

Admit Bearer.

Left: Original shipyard worker's ticket for the launch of the Titanic on 31 May 1911. It was issued to David Moneypenny, a Harland & Wolff painter who worked on Titanic's first class accommodation. The creases in the ticket suggest he had folded it and kept it in his pocket

On 31 May 1911 the Titanic slid down Slipway No. 3 at the Queen's Yard of Harland & Wolff and settled on the waters of the Victoria Channel in Belfast Lough. In her brief life she would be the largest vessel ever built. This shows the port stern entering the water.

Port bow of Titanic, three-quarter profile afloat immediately after launch.

T1 F2 ◖S3 S4 M5 T6 W7 T8 F9 S10 ○ S11 M12 T13 W14 T15 F16 S17 S18 ◗ M19 T20 W21 T22 F23 S24 S25 ● M26 T27 W28 T29 F30

Holidays and Observances

3…First Quarter, 22.04pm   6…Whit Monday   11…Full Moon, 21.50pm   19…Last Quarter, 20.50pm   26…New Moon, 13.19pm

Young girl and boy sitting on a
bathing box in shallow water.

WHIT MONDAY

BEAUTIFUL WEATHER

HUGE HOLIDAY CROWDS

Yesterday was a glorious summer day. With a westerly wind and a falling barometer on Sunday, grave fears were entertained that a change was about to take place in the weather, but early in the morning all doubts were dispelled by the promise of a beautiful day. A cloudless sky and a blazing sun welcomed the pleasure-seekers, and all Dublin and his wife turned out to enjoy the day. It was truly an out-of-doors holiday, and it is very gratifying to be able to state that no serious mishap occurred to mar the pleasures of the multitude. Had it not been for the invasion of our friends from the country, Dublin would have presented a comparatively deserted appearance, as in the early hours of the day almost everyone seemed to be en route to some rendezvous far from the scene of their everyday work. The Baldoyle Races attracted a record crowd, probably one of the largest ever seen on the popular racecourse. The Exhibition at Ballsbridge was also a great centre of interest, the attendance reaching a very high record. All the attractions in this most interesting show were in full swing, and provided for a multitude of people a merry afternoon and evening. In the adjoining jumping enclosure the All-Ireland Athletic Championships were competed for, in the presence of a great crowd of spectators; while every golf course, cricket, and tennis ground was fully occupied by enthusiastic followers of these games. Many people visited the Phoenix Park and Zoological Gardens, while the silvery strands to the north and south of Dublin were thickly dotted with youngsters, who revelled in the pleasures of the day.

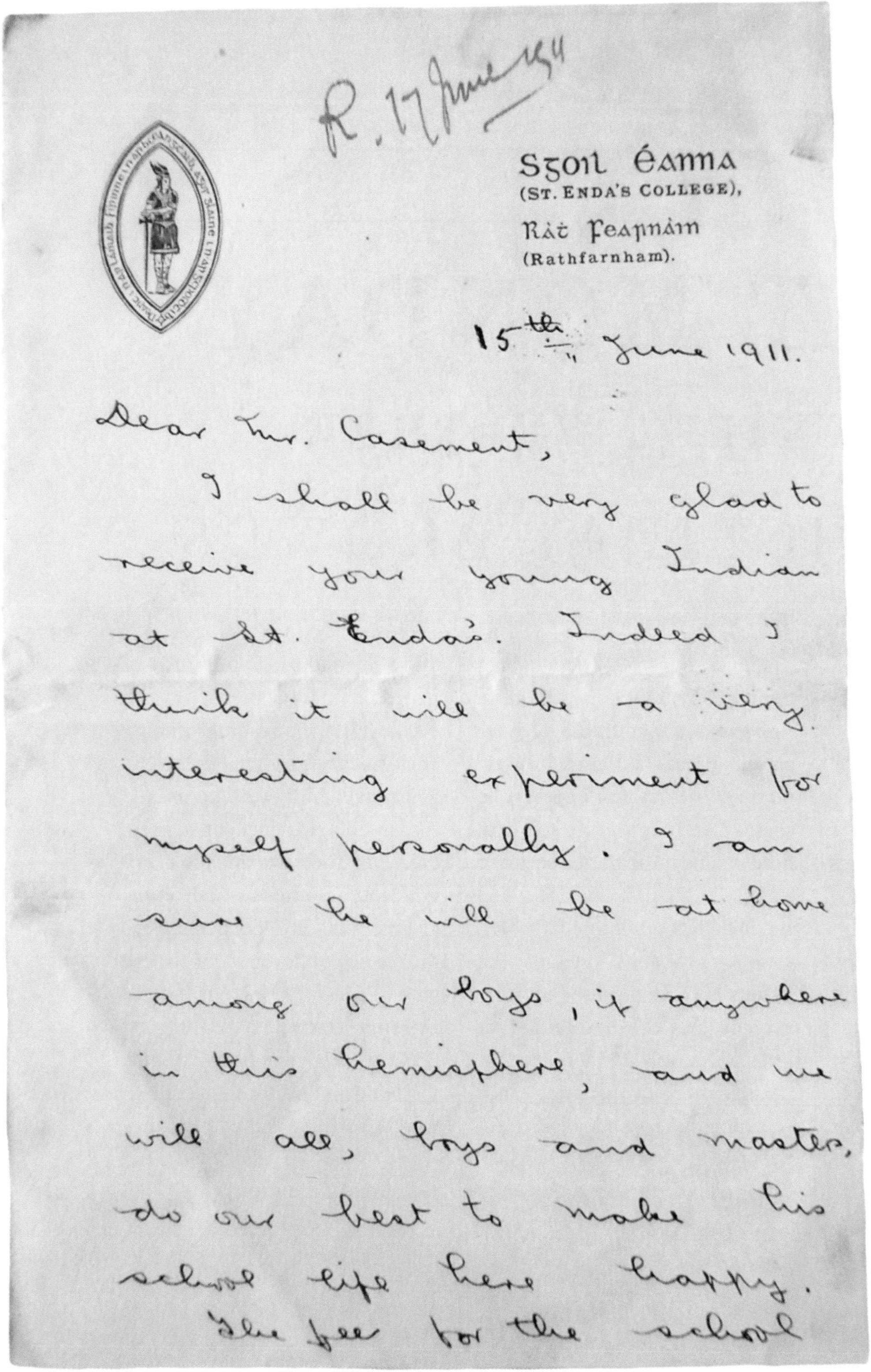

R. 17 June '54

Sgoil Éanna
(ST. ENDA'S COLLEGE),
Ráṫ Ḟearnáin
(Rathfarnham).

15th June 1911.

Dear Mr. Casement,

I shall be very glad to receive your young Indian at St. Enda's. Indeed I think it will be a very interesting experiment for myself personally. I am sure he will be at home among our boys, if anywhere in this hemisphere, and we will all, boys and masters, do our best to make his school life here happy.

The fee for the school

CASEMENT'S 'YOUNG BARBARIAN'

The first and last pages of a letter from Pádraig Pearse to Sir Roger Casement accepting an Indian boy to his school.

The Indian boy was from the Putumayo region of the Amazon. A British diplomat, Casement had been commissioned to investigate reports of abuses of Indian tribes in Putumayo by employees (including British subjects) of the Peruvian Amazon Company. He spent months in the region in 1910. On 17 March he submitted a report to the British government which presented evidence to show that hardship, flogging, starvation and murder were the working conditions for those forced into harvesting rubber in the Peruvian Amazon Company. Casement was knighted by the king in June for his work.

that between us we shall make a great success of this young barbarian. It is work that appeals to me very much.

Sincerely yours

P. H. Pearse.

Casement brought two Indian boys to live with him in London for a period. He made plans to send the younger one to Pearse's school, Scoil Éanna which was situated in The Hermitage in Rathfarnham on 50 acres of parkland. Pearse, a writer and poet, had set up the school because he believed the Irish education system was a 'murder machine' which placed too much emphasis on rote learning. The intervening pages discuss the cost of sending the boy to school (a total of £45 to include pension, laundry, games, supervision, chapel, school cap, football suit, gymnasium suit, kilt for drill and scouting, books and stationery). The final page expresses the hope that 'between us we shall make a great success of this young barbarian'.

IRISH TIMES,
23 JUNE 1911

BURNING
OF THE
UNION
JACK

Coronation Day was celebrated in practically every European capital and in every town of note which possesses a British Colony. Throughout the British Dominions and dependencies the day was signalised by fit rejoicings, and in the United States of America also there were numerous celebrations. President Taft sent a special message to the King expressing the goodwill of his people.

At a *Sinn Féin* meeting, held last evening at the Custom House, Dublin, to protest against Ireland's participation in the Coronation ceremonies, violent speeches were delivered by Mr John McBride, the Countess Markievicz, Dr James McCartan, the Hon. James O'Sullivan, of New York, and others. During the progress of the meeting a man in the crowd caused a good deal of cheering by burning a Union Jack.

VOTES FOR WOMEN

Women's Coronation

PROCESSION

(Five miles long).

Saturday, June 17th,

START 5.30 P.M.

Route via:—TRAFALGAR SQUARE, PALL MALL, PICCADILLY, KNIGHTSBRIDGE.

70 BANDS!
1,000 BANNERS!

THE PROCESSION will march to Kensington, where great meetings in the ROYAL ALBERT HALL and in the EMPRESS ROOMS will be held by the Women's Social and Political Union, at 8.30 p.m., in support of the Woman Suffrage Bill.

Speakers:
Mrs. PANKHURST, Mrs. PETHICK LAWRENCE, Miss VIDA GOLDSTEIN, Miss CHRISTABEL PANKHURST, and others.

Tickets for the Meeting in the EMPRESS ROOMS for Numbered and Reserved Seats, price 2s. 6d. and 1s., can be obtained from The Ticket Secretary, W.S.P.U., 4, Clements Inn, W.C.

For all further plans and particulars read the weekly newspaper VOTES FOR WOMEN. (Price One Penny.) It can be obtained at all newsagents and bookstalls.

Printed by St. Clements Press, Limited, Portugal Street, Kingsway, London, W.C.

Left: Handbill or flyer with details of the Coronation Procession, organised by the Women's Social and Political Union to commemorate the coronation of King George V. The handbill declares the event to be 'The Greatest Procession of Women'. Printed in green and decorated with three clovers, the flyer was aimed specifically at Irish women and invites them to join the 'Irish section' of the march.

Below: Women's Coronation Procession, 1911. During the Women's Coronation Procession, held in London on 17 June 1911, 40,000 women from diverse backgrounds came together to parade their political views. Pipers in national dress headed the Irish women's contingent. Women from Dublin wore Colleen Bawn cloaks in emerald green and carried harps.

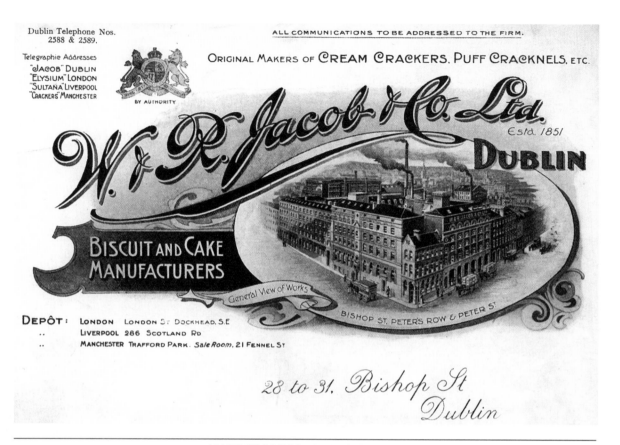

A FEW
BISCUITS
FROM
JACOBS

Another sweet rule is, that any worker late one minute on three occasions in the month is not only fined for each lapse, but is further penalised by being locked out for three days!

If you are caught eating a biscuit, instant dismissal.

* * *

Might I make a suggestion to the women and men of Dublin. If you have not the moral courage to form a Union, get someone to make an application to have the Factory included in the Trades Boards Bill; and don't forget, that if you would pay one penny per week into a trades union for one year – that is, 4s. 4d. per year – the following year you could make Messers. Jacob pay you £4 a year more in wages.

TRADE UNIONS

In 1911 there was high unemployment in Dublin, and poor wages for unskilled workers. The presence of many women and children selling on the streets indicated the precarious nature of employment in the city. The fortunate few who had skilled and semi-skilled work in various trades, such as carpenters, painters and glaziers enjoyed a reasonably secure existence, supported by long-established trade unions. But even here there were problems, as wages had not risen appreciably since the 1870s. Further, many skilled workers were unemployed.

The unskilled labourers of the city, such as dockers, carters and labourers, earned approximately 18 shillings per week for work that was often casual, broken and seasonal. There were estimated to be 24,000 men, one-quarter of the adult males of the city, dependent on such labour and many went for weeks and months without any work at all.

In 1893, the Irish Trade Union Congress had been established to draw together the disparate unions in the city, but it was the employers who won most labour disputes. James Larkin helped to reorganise and radicalise the trade union movement, both in Dublin and nationally. Larkin established the Irish Transport and General Workers' Union in 1909, and by 1911 the union had 18,000 men in its ranks. Women, too, were mobilising. In 1911 the Irish Women Workers' Union was founded with Delia Larkin, James's sister, as its first general secretary.

James Larkin's ambition was to provide representation for unskilled workers, who at this time had no organisation to fight for their rights. He had already organised dock labourers in Belfast and Dublin, and had learned from those experiences how difficult his task was going to be. In 1911 he established the *Irish Worker*, a left-wing newspaper which achieved wide circulation (over 90,000 readers in September 1911).

Larkin had a legendary ability to sway a crowd. Constance Markievicz described his oratory thus:

SITTING THERE, LISTENING TO LARKIN, I REALISED THAT I WAS IN THE PRESENCE OF SOMETHING THAT I HAD NEVER COME ACROSS BEFORE, SOME GREAT PRIMEVAL FORCE RATHER THAN A MAN…IT SEEMED AS IF HIS PERSONALITY CAUGHT UP, ASSIMILATED, AND THREW BACK TO THE VAST CROWD THAT SURROUNDED HIM EVERY EMOTION THAT SWAYED THEM, EVERY PAIN AND JOY THAT THEY HAD EVER FELT MADE ARTICULATE AND SANCTIFIED. ONLY THE GREAT ELEMENTAL FORCE THAT IS IN ALL CROWDS HAD PASSED INTO HIS NATURE FOR EVER. ☞

To the Publisher of "THE IRISH WORKER,"

Offices—CITY PRINTING WORKS, 13 STAFFORD STREET, DUBLIN.

Enter my name on the List of Subscribers to THE IRISH WORKER for one year for which find the sum of ONE SHILLING herewith.

Name_____

Date_____   Address_____

☞ Owing to the difficulty hitherto experienced of securing efficient distribution for a labour journal through the newsagents, THE IRISH WORKER will be delivered FREE in Dublin and Suburbs, while parcels of 12 copies will be sent carriage paid to any part of the country. If single copy to be sent by Post 1s. 6d. should be remitted.

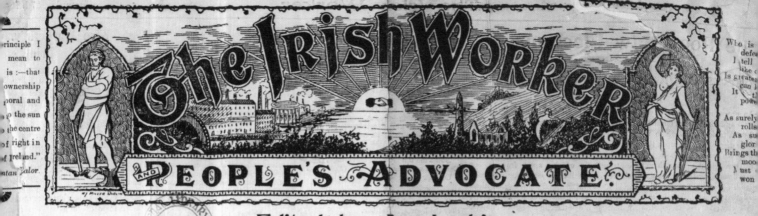

The Irish Worker
and PEOPLE'S ADVOCATE

Edited by Jim Larkin

Vol. I.]   DUBLIN, SATURDAY, MAY 27th, 1911.   [ONE PEN

tform and Principles

rking class of Ireland the Editor
a WORKER makes his bow—not
ble manner, however, but as one
to speak to you and of you with
pride. Too long, aye! far too
we the Irish working people,
and inarticulate. Yes, in the
ld ballad—"Too long have we
ut, now for the future, brave
fear." The Irish Working
letters, good Mr. Printer) are
awaken. They are coming to
uth of the old saying, "He who
free himself must strike the

But what do we mean by Free-
erent individuals, various nations
have their own conception of the
the word Freedom. The dic-
urse, give a definition of the
after reading the dictionary or
one has less understanding of
its application than before
e editorial oracle.

go to the prophets of the
al parties or cliques which we
cursed with. Let us see what
y Freedom—let us take the
duct of the political cauldron—
tes.

their reading of the word means
led Ireland, managed and con-
William O'Brien, M.P.; Maurice
Denraven, Lady Arnott, Lord
rd Barrymore, and last, but not
carde! A land where the
ombeen man, having, with the
pledging the credit of the Irish
been enabled to buy from the
he Barrymores, and the other
merly known as the landlords—
y the grace of, and with the per-

which Griffith is the prophet. A party or
rump, which, while pretending to be Irish of
the Irish, insults the Nation by trying to
foist on it not only imported economics,
based on false principles, but which had the
temerity to advocate the introduction of
foreign capitalists into this sorely-exploited
country. Their chief appeal to the foreign
capitalists was that they (the imported capitalists) would have freedom to employ cheap
Irish labour! No, friend, Arthur, the Irish
capitalist already has too much Freedom to
exploit the worker! of which more anon.

For eleven years these self-appointed prophets and seers have led their army up the
hill and led them down again, and would
continue to so lead them, if allowed, until the
leader was appointed king of Ireland under
the Constitution of 1782. That "Constitution" was a rotten one. The men who
formulated it a bad lot, who sold our country
for their own material benefit, and whose
only regret was that they had not another
country to sell. We want neither imported
economics nor imported capitalists. We
have sufficient capital in the land of Ireland.
We, Irish workers, have the mental and
physical powers to utilise that capital, and
the common-sense section—that is, the working class portion of the Sinn Fein Party, have
realised that now, and will, I feel sure, be
the backbone of the only party to which the
Irish worker should belong—i.e., an Irish
Labour Party.

And now, what of the definition given to
the word Freedom by the party known as the
Nationalist Party? Well, they admit
honestly and openly that they do not believe
in political Freedom, and they know nothing
of economic Freedom! They state logically
enough, I admit, that they are a party bound
together for one purpose—namely, the accom-
plishment of a movement to achieve self-
government for Ireland; and that, as far as
is humanly possible, they are not going to
allow Freedom to anybody, either to think or

nation, nor the king, governors, or representatives of any other nation. That all such
persons are interlopers and trespassers on
this our land, and that we are determined to
accomplish not only National Freedom, but
a greater thing—Individual Freedom—Freedom from military and political slavery,
such as we suffer under at present, but also
from a more degraded slavery, economic or
wage slavery! How, then, are we to achieve
Freedom and Liberty?

To accomplish political and economic
Freedom we must have our own party!
There is no difficulty whatever about that.
That party means the People—all men and
women who are willing to work and build
up an Irish Nation! That party must have
principles! And, forget not, workers, that
principles are greater than persons! It was
persons who sold this Nation in the past!
Put your trust in no man, you will therefore
never be confounded. Stand by your principles. Let them be as fixed as the sun.

Yes, true Freedom is to be in earnest to
make others free! Such then, is the policy
of this paper. Such are its principles—
broad—based upon the people's will!

Bide your time; the man is breaking
    Bright with Freedom's blessed ray,
Millions from their trance awaking,
    Soon shall stand in firm array.
Man shall fetter man no longer,
    Liberty shall march sublime,
Every moment makes us stronger,
    Calm and thoughtful, bide your time.

Bide your time, one false step taken
    Perils all you yet have done,
Undismayed, erect, unshaken,
    Watch and wait and all is won.
'Tis not by a rash endeavour,
    Man can e'er to greatness climb,
Would you win your rights for ever?
    Firm, unshrinking, bide your time.

Bide your time, your wirst trangression
    Were to strike and strike in vain,
He whose arm would smite oppression,
    Must not need to strike again.
Danger makes the brave man steady,
    Rashness is the coward's crime,

need never work; and, instead of being
called a pauper, would be pampered and
feted. Civic receptions would be offered
by Irish Nationalists, so-called; Unionists,
place-hunters, and other disloyal Irishmen
would actually fall down and lick his boots.
The speaker also pointed out the publican
element in the Nationalist life was responsible for a lot of the toadyism that was ram-
part in their midst. Men who were elected
on the understanding that they would not
present a loyal address, after election were
falling over themselves to do so. Quote the
case of the present Lord Mayor, the late Lord
Mayor, and tried and true Nationalists, who
even refused the king of England civic hos-
pitality, because they dare not be men and
act as they would like to act—go down to
another public board and vote the address
they had previously refused. And the same
spirit of toadyism permeates all public life in
this country.

He quoted a letter from a Dublin evening
paper, written by a member of the police,
wherein it was stated a man could not get
promotion in the D.M.P., unless he was a
time-server or kicked off with the right foot;
in fact, if a man changed his opinions, and,
still better, his creed, to suit the parties in
power, not only in the police, but in many
other Government offices, as well as in private firms, it would be conducive to one's
own advancement.

Just at this point in the address, whether
the question of changing one's religion for
promotion, or the statement that one required
to kick off with the right foot seemed to
affect the officer in charge of the police (Inspector Kiernan, I understand)—these statements had evidently touched him on the
raw. He suddenly turned to his men,
12 or 14 in number, saying : "Come on, by
God! I'll stop him ; I'll pull him down !"
And, rushing through the crowd, like a man
who had lost his senses, he rushed up to the
waggon whereon Larkin was speaking, and
shouted out: "Say that again and I'll take
you down ; and you also attacked the king."

It was a touching sight. Here was the
representative of Law and Order, the man
who was responsible for the peace, actually
trying to create a breach of the peace. Everyone in the crowd agreeing with the speaker,
applauding his points ; not a dissentient

Questions We Wo
Answered.

To LADY ABERDEEN—Wh
posters advertising the Ui Bree
Exhibition printed? Would
say they were designed and p
row, near London?

To CAPTAIN CUFFE (or Cap
forget which is right—How
are working in the cabinet wor
How many imported blacklegs
imported Israelites? Is the
The Countess of Dysart home

Will Captain Snuff or Cou
much of the investor's money
the Kilkenny Woodworks ur
ance of the late imported m
why Hunter resigned; and is
ger an Irish product?

How many Trades Unionis
in the Kilkenny Woodworke
Czar of all the Kilkenny
satisfied with his imported
imported blacklegs? And,
Otway Cuffe. Can we trade
in the "Island of the Blest
allow us to work in the Isle w
may we ask, with due deter
being meek and lowly of birt
the gentle knights and lad
organised (or who get the cred
sed," sweating exhibition—ho
firms exhibiting pay the rece
wages and employ Trades Un

Should this not be called the
the best"—the free-labour
No, my genteels, the Irish w
want Irish industry built u
scab labour.

How many Trades Union
Alderman Cotton, M.P., emplo
city as managing-director of t
How many of the stoves exh
company are made in Ireland
machinery; how much im
how many imported brickla
Gas Company imported, so as
gas workers out of their emp
wer see Gas Co's. last Balance

How many machines has Si

☞ The response to Larkin's union from employers was trenchant. William Martin Murphy was the most prominent businessman in the city. He owned railways, tramways, Clery's department store, the Imperial Hotel and, critically, the *Irish Independent* newspaper. He was at the heart of the reaction against the growing militancy of labour, and established the Dublin Employer's Federation in 1912. Conflict seemed inevitable. Across the city there was a rise in labour disputes.

In 1911 there occurred a wave of strikes. The bakers' union engaged in a strike which was the culmination of two decades of disputes over work practices and pay. They lost. A railway strike also ended in abject defeat for workers who had taken on the Great Southern and Western Railway Companies. Some disputes brought minor gains, but the presence of a huge surplus of unskilled workers undermined union efforts. The battle was growing increasingly desperate as the city moved towards its greatest labour conflict, the 1913 Lockout. ❋

NO. 1. FOURTH YEAR

A BROADSIDE

FOR JUNE, 1911.
PUBLISHED MONTHLY BY E. C. YEATS AT THE CUALA PRESS,
CHURCHTOWN, DUNDRUM, COUNTY DUBLIN.
SUBSCRIPTION TWELVE SHILLINGS A YEAR POST FREE.

NELSON STREET

There is hardly a mouthful of air
In the room where the breakfast is set,
For the blind is still down tho' it's late,
And the curtains are redolent yet
Of tobacco smoke, stale from last night.
There's the little bronze teapot, and there
The rashers and eggs on the plate,
And the sleepy canary, a hen
Starts faintly her chirruping tweet,
And I know could she speak she would say:
'Hullo there— what's wrong with the light?
Draw the blind up, let's look at the day.'

I see that it's Monday again,
For the man with the organ is there;
Every Monday he comes to the street
(Lest I, or the bird there, should miss
Our count of monotonous days)
With his reed-organ, wheezy and sweet,
And stands by the window and plays
'There's a Land that is fairer than this.'

Seumas O'Sullivan.

300 copies only.

S1 S2 ◖M3 T4 W5 T6 F7 S8 S9 M10 ○ T11 W12 T13 F14 S15 S16 M17 T18 ◗ W19 T20 F21 S22 S23 M24 ● T25 W26 T27 F28 S29 S30 M31

Holidays and Observances

1…First Quarter, 9.20am   7…Old Midsummer Day   11…Full Moon, 0.53pm   15…St Swithin's   19…Last Quarter, 5.31am   25…New Moon, 8.12pm

THE ROYAL VISIT

SCENES AT THE LANDING OF THEIR MAJESTIES

STATE PROCESSION TO DUBLIN

PRESENTATION OF ADDRESSES AND REPLIES EN ROUTE

TRIUMPHAL MARCH THROUGH THE CITY

NEW COLLEGE OF SCIENCE OPENED AND TWO KNIGHTHOODS CONFERRED

A VISIT TO TRINITY

THEIR MAJESTIES AT THE PHOENIX PARK RACES

SCENES OF PAGENTRY, COLOUR AND LIFE

OVERFLOWING STREETS; BRILLIANT ILLUMINATIONS

THE KING'S BUSY SUNDAY

VISIT TO MAYNOOTH AND OTHER PUBLIC ENGAGEMENTS

Their majesties King George V and Queen Mary, with the Prince of Wales and Princess Mary, landed at Kingstown punctually at the scheduled time on Saturday morning, and were enthusiastically welcomed by the thousands assembled.

The Royal procession by road to Dublin was marked at all parts along the route by spontaneous and cordial demonstrations of welcome from the dense crowds everywhere assembled, and the castle was reached at 12.20pm.

As their Majesties entered the Royal Barge from the Royal Yacht Victoria and Albert a Royal salute was fired by the fleet. Their Majesties who were greeted with enthusiastic and prolonged cheers from the multitude were received by their Excellencies the Lord Lieutenant and the Countess of Aberdeen and the high officers of State. His Excellence presented the Chairman of the Kingstown Urban District Council, and a loyal address of welcome from the Council, to their Majesties was read by Dr. Sherlock Vaughan, Town Clerk. His Majesty, in the course of his reply, said they desired to take the earliest opportunity of coming among their Irish people, in whose welfare their interest was deep and abiding.

The newly crowned King George V and his wife Queen Mary in Dublin. The king is pressing the electric button to open the door of his carriage.

The King and Queen, accompanied by the Prince of Wales and Princess Mary, made their State entry into Dublin on Saturday. Their Majesties disembarked from the Royal yacht at Kingstown Harbour, and their processional drive to and through Dublin was attended by scenes of great enthusiasm and manifestations of loyalty. In reply to addresses of welcome, the King expressed his deep and abiding interest in the welfare of his Irish people. At the Royal College of Science, which he formally declared open, the King Knighted Mr. Thomas Manly Deane, Joint Architect of the building, and announced a similar honour for Professor Hartley, Dean of Faculty of the College. Their Majesties afterwards visited Trinity college, where two addresses were presented. A visit was paid in the afternoon to Phoenix Park Races, and subsequently Their Majesties took afternoon tea with the Lord Lieutenant and the Countess of Aberdeen at the Viceregal Lodge.

On the way back to the Castle, Their Majesties paid a brief visit to the Lord Iveagh Play Centre. The Prince of Wales and Princess Mary were present in the afternoon at Dublin University Boat Club Regatta.

Yesterday morning the King and Queen, the Prince of Wales and Princess Mary attended Divine Service in St. Patrick's Cathedral. The sermon was preached by the Primate. In the afternoon Their Majesties drove by motor to Maynooth College, and on their return inspected the Veterans in the Royal Hospital at Kilmainham.

Below: The University Club situated on St Stephen's Green took the unusual step of allowing women into some specific areas of the Club on the day of the king's arrival. Their minutes read: 'With reference to Resolution No. 9 of 1st May the Committee decided that on Saturday the 8th July, the day of the King's arrival, ladies accompanied by members may be admitted to lunch and afternoon tea at the Club, all arrangements and details being left to the Coffee Room Committee. The General Committee also suggested that the guests may be brought to the Coffee Room, the Reading Room and the Library.'

With reference to Res.ⁿ No 9 of 1.ˢᵗ May, the Committee decided that on Saturday the 8.ᵗʰ July, the day of the King's arrival, ladies accompanied by members may be admitted to lunch & afternoon tea at the Club, all arrangements and details being left to the Coffee Room Committee. The General Committee also suggested that the guests may be brought to the Coffee Room, the Reading Room & the Library.

Right: Invitation to afternoon party at the vice-regal lodge on Tuesday, 11 July 1911, to Mr and Mrs Alfred B. Coyle.

Alfred B. Coyle (37) was an insurance broker. His wife of two years Florence (21) had recently had a son, also called Alfred Bernard. They lived at 54 Highfield Road, Rathmines.

The Lord Chamberlain is commanded by Their Majesties to invite

Mr. and Mrs Alfred B. Coyle

to an Afternoon Party at the Vice Regal Lodge on Tuesday the 11th July 1911, from 3.30 to 5.30 o'clock.

The Castle, Dublin.

Morning Dress.

Programme of the
Royal Progress.

'To-day Another English Monarch Visits Ireland…' Nationalist Women's Association protest against the royal visit.

❀ Nationalist Women's ❀ Association.

To-day
Another English Monarch visits Ireland.

When
will Ireland regain the Legislature which is by everyone granted to be her mere right?

Never !
As long as Irish men and women stand in the streets of Dublin to cheer the King of England, and crawl to those who oppress and rob them.

God Save Ireland !

Right: 'The Royal Visit' protest pamplet issued by the Socialist Party of Ireland.

Left: Crowds of people line the royal processional route in College Green, Dublin in July 1911. There is a viewing stand in front of the Bank of Ireland and the façade of the building is decorated for the visit. Garlands and bunting are also displayed along the street.

Socialist Party in Ireland
(DUBLIN BRANCH).

THE ROYAL VISIT.

" The great appear great to us, only because we are on our knees:
LET US RISE."

FELLOW-WORKERS—As you are aware from reading the daily and weekly newspapers, we are about to be blessed with a visit from King George V. Knowing from previous experience of Royal Visits, as well as from the Coronation orgies of the past few weeks, that the occasion will be utilised to make propaganda on behalf of royalty and aristocracy against the oncoming forces of democracy and National freedom, we desire to place before you some few reasons why you should unanimously refuse to countenance this visit, or to recognise it by your presence at its attendant processions or demonstrations. We appeal to you as workers, speaking to workers, whether your work be that of the brain or of the hand—manual or mental toil—it is of you and your children we are thinking; it is your cause we wish to safeguard and foster.

The future of the working class requires that all political and social positions should be open to all men and women; that all privileges of birth or wealth be abolished, and that every man or woman born into this land should have an equal opportunity to attain to the proudest position in the land. The Socialist demands that the only birthright necessary to qualify for public office should be the birthright of our common humanity. Believing as we do that there is nothing on earth more sacred than humanity, we deny all allegiance to this institution of royalty, and hence can only regard the visit of the King as adding fresh fuel to the fire of hatred with which we regard the plundering institutions of which he is the representative. Let the capitalist and landlord class flock to exalt him; he is theirs; in him they see embodied the idea of caste and class; they glorify him and exalt his importance that they might familiarise the public mind with the conception of political inequality, knowing well that a people mentally poisoned by the adulation of royalty can never attain to that spirit of self-reliant democracy necessary for the attainment of social freedom. The mind accustomed to political kings can easily be reconciled to social kings—capitalist kings of the workshop, the mill, the railway, the ships and the docks. Thus coronation and king's visits are by our astute, never-sleeping masters made into huge Imperialist propagandist campaigns in favour of political and social schemes against democracy. But if our masters and rulers are sleepless in their schemes against us, so we, rebels against their rule, must never sleep in our appeal to our fellows to maintain publicly our belief in the dignity of our class—in the ultimate sovereignty of those who labour.

P.T.O.

A group of spectators stand on wagons to watch the military review which was held at the Fifteen Acres in the Phoenix Park , Dublin, during the royal visit, on 11 July 1911.

f   f   d   e   b c   a   B

The Gumbleton Bequest

The Botanic Gardens received a rare collection of books owing to the death of dilettante and enthusiastic gardener William Edward Gumbleton. He lived on his estate 'Belgrove' on Great Island in Cork Harbour where he grew rare plants and built up a valuable library. Frederick Moore, the curator of the Gardens, recalled W.E. Gumbleton's first visit to the Gardens shortly after he was appointed at the age of 22: 'In front of the Curvilinear Range, Mr Gumbleton denounced a plant…as "a Tush Plant", his term for any plant he did not like, and proceeded to beat it to bits with his umbrella…I was too timid to do more than mildly remonstrate, and bemoan the loss of a recently arrived plant'. Moore and Gumbleton became friends and the Botanic Gardens was the beneficiary of rare books, including the exquisitely illustrated *Flora Graeca*, from his library in July.

◖ T1 W2 T3 F4 S5 S6 M7 T8 W9 ○ T10 F11 S12 S13 M14 T15 W16 ◗ T17 F18 S19 S20 M21 T22 W23 ● T24 F25 S26 S27 M28 T29 W30 ◖ T31

Holidays and Observances

1…First Quarter, 11.29pm   7…August Bank Holiday   10…Full Moon, 2.55am   14…Old Lammas Day

17…Last Quarter, 0.11pm   24…New Moon, 4.14am   31…First Quarter, 4.21pm

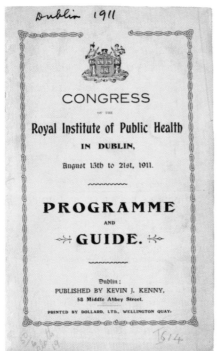

In 1911, the population of Dublin was affected by child mortality, tuberculosis, typhoid, dysentery and other diseases mainly caused by overcrowding, unsanitary living conditions, poor nutrition and lack of hygiene. Families were large: over a third of married women in 1911 (36%) had seven children or more. The death rate in Dublin per 1,000 was 22.3; in London it was just 15.6. Childbirth was life-threatening for many mothers, with geographical location and social class the major determining factors in mortality. Babies born in urban areas were almost twice as vulnerable as those born in the countryside: the urban infant mortality rate was 150 per 1,000 live births, and rural mortality was 74. A baby born into the family of a labourer was seventeen times more likely to die within a year than was the child of a professional.

Life Expectancy in Ireland 1911 — Men: 53.6 • Women: 54.1 —

Hundreds of delegates from around the world convened at the Royal Dublin Society in Ballsbridge for the Congress of the Royal Institute for Public Health which ran from 15 to 21 August.

Lady Aberdeen, Ishbel Gordon, wife of the lord lieutenant, was influential in establishing the Women's National Health Association, which operated mother and baby clubs in Dublin from 1908, providing medical and practical nutritional and hygiene advice to mothers. There were home visits from nurses, and cheap pasteurised milk was provided. These clubs, where they existed, had caused a considerable decrease in child mortality, but some census returns show that there were still critical levels. Marjorie Dixon, who lived in a single room in Buckingham Street with her husband, five children and a nurse-child, had given birth to thirteen children, only six of whom survived. Another of Lady Aberdeen's initiatives was the fight against tuberculosis or phthisis (consumption), which was causing almost 12,000 deaths per year, mainly among young adults in the 15- to 25-year age group.

Germ theory was still poorly understood, and some people believed that 'the white plague' was hereditary. The National Association for the Prevention of Tuberculosis and the Women's National Health Association launched a campaign of education and eradication, using travelling wagons to disseminate information. Some unkind wags referred to Lady Aberdeen as 'Lady Microbe', mocking her zeal in the eradication of germs. However, these initiatives had considerable success, and, between 1905 and 1918, with better economic and social conditions, improved standards of domestic hygiene and greater public awareness of the dangers of infection, the death toll from tuberculosis was reduced by about a quarter.

Small hospitals were established in every corner of the city, run by religious orders or charities, and funded by benefactors and philanthropists, with increasing contributions from the state. The Mater Hospital was run by the Catholic Sisters of Mercy, while the Rotunda, the Coombe and the South Dublin Lying-in Hospital in Holles Street were designed to improve the appallingly high levels of death in childbirth. Most wealthy and middle-class women stayed at home to have their babies; the lying-in hospitals were intended for those who lived

The 'War on consumption' is waged on Rutland Square.

For leaving a sick-bed quickly — for keeping you well always — there is no other tonic like

Hall's Wine. Coughs, colds, that "run-down," "out-of-sorts" feeling—all are driven out by the new life-force which Hall's Wine sends coursing through your veins. An immediate nerve tonic, a replenisher of the blood-supply, Hall's Wine has stood the medical and home-use test of 25 years. Prevents influenza. Relieves chronic bronchitis. *To-day* get one of the new 3/6 extra-large bottles of

Hall's Wine

The Delicious Wine Tonic and Marvellous Restorative.

in poverty. The census return for patients in the Mater Hospital in 1911 lists illnesses such as breast and abdominal tumours, goitre, gallstones, appendicitis, hernia, fractures and varicose veins. Mental illness could result in incarceration in one of the city's asylums, or in the workhouse, although many mentally ill people lived at home with their families. The return for the Richmond Female Lunatic Asylum in Upper Grangegorman lists 900 patients as suffering from such illnesses as melancholia, paranoia, mania, dementia, imbecility and epilepsy, then wrongly believed to be a psychiatric problem.

The doctors in Dublin in 1911 had graduated from the many medical schools in the city including the Cecilia Street

Doctors and nurses outside the Rotunda Hospital, Parnell Square holding newborn babies, patients of the hospital.

Medical School and the Royal College of Surgeons. A number of nurses' homes were built across the city, including one adjoining Eccles Street, near the Mater Hospital, which opened in 1903. South of the river, Portobello House, once a hotel, later an asylum for blind women, was, by 1911, a nursing home. And on nearby Camden Row was an early hospice opened in 1904 by Colonel Gascoigne Trench, called unequivocally the 'Rest for the Dying'. ✳

INSANITY   IRELAND

Proportion of Number of Insane Under Care To every 1000 of Population
(In Asylums and Workhouses)

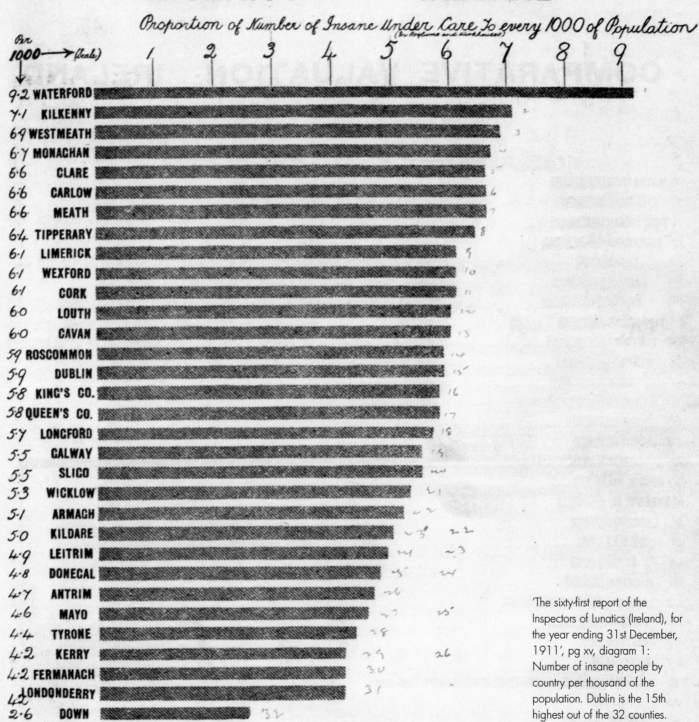

Per 1000 → (Scale)	1	2	3	4	5	6	7	8	9

Value	County	Rank
9·2	WATERFORD	1
7·1	KILKENNY	2
6·9	WESTMEATH	3
6·7	MONAGHAN	4
6·6	CLARE	5
6·6	CARLOW	6
6·6	MEATH	7
6·4	TIPPERARY	8
6·1	LIMERICK	9
6·1	WEXFORD	10
6·1	CORK	11
6·0	LOUTH	12
6·0	CAVAN	13
5·9	ROSCOMMON	14
5·9	DUBLIN	15
5·8	KING'S CO.	16
5·8	QUEEN'S CO.	17
5·7	LONGFORD	18
5·5	GALWAY	19
5·5	SLIGO	20
5·3	WICKLOW	21
5·1	ARMAGH	22
5·0	KILDARE	23
4·9	LEITRIM	24
4·8	DONEGAL	25
4·7	ANTRIM	26
4·6	MAYO	27
4·4	TYRONE	28
4·2	KERRY	29
4·2	FERMANAGH	30
4·2	LONDONDERRY	31
2·6	DOWN	32

'The sixty-first report of the Inspectors of Lunatics (Ireland), for the year ending 31st December, 1911', pg xv, diagram 1: Number of insane people by country per thousand of the population. Dublin is the 15th highest out of the 32 counties.

Sir, —For the information of those whom it may interest, will you kindly afford me the courtesy of your columns to state that the shade temperature here today reached 80 degrees, and in the sun at 2 pm it stood at 119 degrees. For the corresponding date last year the figures were 69 and 99 degrees respectively.

This is the highest temperature I have recorded this season, except the 13th July, when the shade temperature registered 81 degrees, and in the sun it rose to 120 degrees.

During the month of August last year the highest temperature I have noted in the shade was 72 degrees and this occurred only on one date, the 10th. For 1909 the highest temperature here for the month of August was precisely the same, 72 degrees, which was registered on the 12th of that month.—

Yours, etc.,

J. SCALLAN. Dromin Junction, Co. Louth.

F → C

80° → 26°

119° → 48°

IRISH INDEPENDENT,
20 AUGUST 1911

TOWNSHIP PARKS

Through the generosity of the Earl of Pembroke the people of the Pembroke township have been provided with a very pretty Park. In the City of Dublin such open spaces are rather numerous, but in the townships there have been so far no parks of any considerable size. Pembroke can now boast of one of the best. The donor richly merits the gratitude expressed to him at the opening ceremony on Saturday.

IRISH TIMES,
21 AUGUST 1911

HERBERT PARK OPENED BY THE LORD LIEUTENANT

LORD PEMBROKE THANKED

On Saturday afternoon the Lord Lieutenant formally opened Herbert Park, in the Pembroke district of Dublin. His Excellency was accompanied by the Countess of Aberdeen, and attended by Lieutenant E.T. Warner, A.D.C. The opening ceremony took place in the presence of a large gathering of prominent residents in the district and of delegates to the Public Health Congress who were specially invited by the Pembroke Urban Council.

The Chairman of the Council, Mr. Charles P. O'Neill, J.P., who presided, opened the proceedings with a statement regarding the park. At the outset, he said that in honouring them by their presence there the Lord Lieutenant and the Countess of Aberdeen had again shown the active and sympathetic interest they took in the welfare of the people of Ireland, and in heartily thanking Their Excellencies he was giving expression to the sentiments of his fellow members of the Pembroke Council and of the Pembroke Committee, who had co-operated with him to further the object they had in view that day. They had also expressed a desire to join with him and their fellow-citizens in welcoming their distinguished guests, the delegates and members of the Public Health Congress.

EARL OF PEMBROKE'S GIFT

That park (Mr. O'Neill continued), which had an area of 35 acres, had been granted to the Pembroke Urban Council by the present Earl of Pembroke in commemoration of the coming of age of his eldest son, Lord Herbert, on the understanding that the park was to be laid out and thenceforth be maintained by the Urban Council solely for the purpose of a public park, to be called and known as Herbert

Park, for the benefit of the district and the neighbourhood.

PUBLIC THANKS

The Pembroke Council had already passed resolutions thanking Lord Pembroke, and he was desired by the Council to express in public the best thanks of the Council and of the residents of the district for the inestimable benefit conferred on them by Lord Pembroke by the granting of Herbert Park. (Applause.) Few things, if any, conduce more to the good health of a district than parks and open spaces. (Hear, hear.) He ventured, therefore, to say that it was fitting and appropriate that the Opening of Herbert Park should take place during the present successful session of the Public Health Congress, and to hope that it would serve to give a further impetus to the very successful Town Planning Exhibition held in a place a short distance from there, for which the Countess of Aberdeen had been responsible.

It was right to mention that while Lord Pembroke had provided that splendid park in the principal residential part of Pembroke district, he had thoughtfully remembered the poor man as well as the rich man, for he had also granted for the use of the working classes a park of equal, if not larger, extent, which was much appreciated by them.(Applause.)

On the conclusion of the opening ceremony an enjoyable garden party was held, affording the guests an opportunity of inspecting the park. The band of the Royal Irish Constabulary and Pembroke Brass Band played during the afternoon.

A demonstration by the Pembroke Fire Brigade, under Captain Hutson, with their petrol motor fire engine of the Hatfield pattern (Merryweather patent), was extremely interesting. The motor ran quickly into the park, pulled up at the lake, and in the short space of 27 seconds had three jets of water going to a height of 120 feet, with 140 lbs. pressure to the square inch. This fully illustrated the Brigade's rapidity of action in case of fire. Then followed a series of large high pressure deluge jets, some of which attained the height of 220 feet with 170 lbs. pressure to the square inch. The spectators expressed themselves highly pleased with the display.

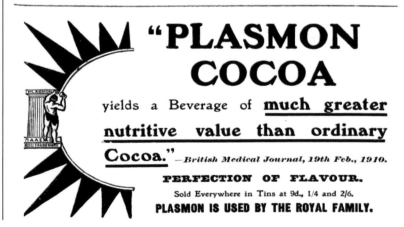

THE SUBURBS

The growth of residential areas away from the central shopping, commercial and industrial core of a city was a common phenomenon across Europe in the nineteenth and early twentieth centuries. Dublin was no exception. The city had been surrounded by outlying villages—Kingstown, Donnybrook, Chapelizod, Malahide and many more—for several centuries. By 1911 significant change in the pattern of Dublin life had drawn such villages closer into the life of the city.

The nineteenth century saw a steady move to suburbs such as Rathmines, Monkstown and Blackrock by many wealthy Dubliners. Not all who could afford to left for the suburbs: for example, Fitzwilliam Square and Merrion Square on the south side of the city remained the preserve of the wealthy. This was a world of doctors, lawyers, senior civil servants and army officers. The old fashionable districts of the north side, however, were almost entirely abandoned. Among the starkest examples were the great buildings of Henrietta Street, Mountjoy Square and Parnell Square which were now tenements, occupied by poor families in packed and derelict conditions.

The suburbs were not uniformly affluent or even prosperous. Nonetheless, it was clear that the relocation was initiated by the professional classes, who sought residence at a distance from the polluted, overcrowded city centre. It was equally clear that the loss of many of its more affluent and influential inhabitants had a detrimental affect on the development of life in the inner city. In this respect, Ireland reflected trends happening in many other European cities.

Middle-class families sought houses which reflected their new-found status, houses which could not in any case be provided within the city confines. Development of the suburbs was driven by businessmen and property developers, as in the case of Rathmines, or independent landowners, as in the case of Pembroke, which was the project of the earl of Pembroke. From the 1860s, the inner suburbs of Rathmines and Pembroke grew year after year. By 1911 Rathmines and Pembroke accounted for up to half of the suburban population of Dublin, with Rathmines alone being home to 38,000 people.

Certain suburbs were favoured by various trades or professions. Kilmainham was filled with workers from the railway companies who had engineering and other plants in the area, while there was also a considerable military presence, and Clontarf was home to clerks and salesmen. Drumcondra had a lot of civil servants and a significant presence of priests, monks and theology students through the presence of All Hallows and Clonliffe seminaries.

There was, however, considerable diversity of occupation in particular streets, like Dunville Avenue in Rathmines. Served by a railway station, it might have been considered the quintessential suburban street, and it did indeed have its share of civil servants, clerks and accountants. However, it was also home to diverse others, including a singing teacher and her two daughters, one of whom was an actress, a cinematograph operator, students, and a 68-year old single woman who said she was of no religious persuasion and refused to divulge any information on the matter to the enumerator.

In other suburbs, there was a significant element of religious clustering. In Clontarf, about one-tenth of the population was

Presbyterian and Methodist, and more than one-quarter was Church of Ireland, choosing to live close to the schools and churches which serviced their denomination. In many outlying suburbs, Protestants, Methodists and Presbyterians were over-represented in proportion to their overall numbers in the city.

In Monkstown, the 1911 census shows the Catholic population to be in a minority. In other outlying suburbs, such as Blackrock, Glasthule and Kingstown, the non-Catholic population was one-third, or greater. This was despite the fact that Catholics constituted 83% of Dublin's population in 1911.

In all, ten independent townships grew up around Dublin, profoundly affecting life in the existing villages, most of which were radically changed. The development of railways and tramways facilitated the emergence of a pioneering group of commuters, who continued to work in the city but escaped to their suburban retreats out of office hours.

The geography of the city was becoming more important than ever before, not simply in terms of its physical manifestation, but also in terms of status. Suburbs took on a meaning rooted in expressions of class and social standing. A variety of reasons—available land, available resources, available transport, lower rates—determined that the suburbs to the south of the city were generally the most prestigious. A new suburban lifestyle emerged.

Junction at Rathmines, Dublin.

Many constructed a leisure world around golf clubs, tennis clubs and bridge schools. Kingstown (now Dún Laoghaire), for example, was fashionable for its yachting and other maritime activities, including swimming at the men's only Forty Foot, a small natural harbour in Sandycove. Other suburbs made the most of the growth in local tourism and leisure outings. Malahide had been home to the Grand Hotel since 1835, while holiday homes were built at St James's Terrace and Killeen Terrace. In 1910 a new hotel and sanatorium was opened on the River Liffey by the Lucan Hydropathic Spa company.

The suburbs were not merely retreats for the middle classes. A significant working-class population lived cheek-by-jowl with their newly prosperous neighbours, not to mention the number of servants which many kept. Significant working-class populations in the Ringsend and Irishtown areas of Pembroke had to endure bad housing, bad sanitation and bad health. Most suburban Dubliners kept at least one servant, though many kept several.

While suburbanisation dispersed the population across the county, Dublin remained rural across great sweeps of its territory. County Dublin had been created before 1200 and was the third smallest of all Irish counties—only Carlow and Louth were smaller—comprising only 922 square kilometres. North County Dublin remained profoundly rural in aspect. From the northern village of Balbriggan, down through Skerries, Rush and Malahide, and across Swords and Donabate, Dublin was as dependent on agriculture as were much of the midlands and west of Ireland. The hinterland of Dublin which stretched down from the mountains in the south of the county and across west Dublin to Rathcoole was also dominated by agriculture.

This was a world of land stewards, farmers, farm labourers, farmer-publicans, grooms, poulterers and meat merchants. Dublin was an imperial capital city, but it was also a country town. ✵

IRISH INDEPENDENT,
25 AUGUST 1911

OUR CLOCKS

GREENWICH TIME IN IRELAND

Mr. Field, M.P., at yesterday's meeting of the Dublin Port and Docks Board, when told that the Board had passed a resolution in favour of the adoption of Greenwich time in Ireland, said he disagreed entirely with such a decision. The natural law as to time, based on the sun's passage over the meridian, could not, he said, be altered by any resolution of that Board, or of any Chamber of Commerce. He protested against taking Irish time from Greenwich. The chairman (M.W. Wallace, J.P.) said he would mark a letter from the Dublin Co. Council signifying that body's acceptance of the adoption of Greenwich time, "Noted with approval."

"And mark it Mr. Field dissenting," said Mr. Field, M.P., who afterwards handed in notice of motion to the effect that the resolution passed on June 15 advocating the change of Irish to Greenwich time be rescinded, as it is opposed to the law of nature and the geographical position of Ireland.

F1 S2 S3 M4 T5 W6 T7 ○ F8 S9 S10 M11 T12 W13 T14 ☽ F15 S16 S17 M18 T19 W20 T21 ● F22 S23 S24 M25 T26 W27 T28 F29 ☾ S30

Holidays and Observances

8…Full Moon, 3.57pm   15…Last Quarter, 5.51pm   22…New Moon, 2.37pm   24…Autumn Commences, 4.18am

29…Michaelmas Day.   30…First Quarter 11.08am

Girls' Senior Hockey Team, 1911/12, Wesley College. Wesley College educated Methodist boys in Dublin and, in September 1911, it opened its doors to girls who desired 'to secure such training as will fit them for professional and business careers'. The college purchased No. 110 St Stephen's Green as a girls' hostel. It had formerly been known as The Epworth Club, a boarding house for young Epworth businessmen coming to Dublin, which had ceased to serve its purpose. Six boarder girls and fifteen day girls joined the 175 boys already in the college.

Education

Free primary education after 1831, and the introduction of compulsory education for children between the ages of six and fourteen in 1892, ensured that all the children of Dublin had access to a basic level of education, at least in theory. The reality was that poverty in working-class Dublin ensured that the majority of its children left formal education before finishing national school. With many children forced to support their families by selling wares or begging on the streets, the poorest children often gained only a patchy education.

The result was that in schools such as Synge Street Christian Brothers' school, the numbers dwindled significantly as the classes got older. Crucially, however, the national schools did promote basic literacy, for most. Away from the national school system a range of different private schools prospered across the city, like the German High School at Wellington

Place, Donnybrook. Some were grind schools dedicated to preparing students for the civil service examinations.

Pádraig Pearse founded Scoil Éanna (St Enda's) school in 1909 in opposition to the examination-orientated 'murder-machine' of the state system, and designed a curriculum intended to promote a rounded awareness of Gaelic language, culture and history.

In Clontarf, the Hibernian Marine School catered for day-students and 60 boarders and was initially established for boys from seafaring families who were orphans, or from families unable to afford fees. Also on the north side, in nearby Artane, hundreds of children lived at the Artane Industrial School under the supervision of the Christian Brothers. Similar industrial schools operated in various parts of the city; these included St Anne's on Booterstown Avenue and the various O'Brien's industrial schools. Many of the students, as we now know, suffered terrible abuse and neglect at the hands of some of their 'carers'.

Attempts to provide non-denominational secondary education, such as existed, were opposed by the churches. Secondary schools in Dublin were privately run, divided by religion and, apart from Christian Brothers' schools, were fee-paying. As well as the fees from students, the schools were funded by the state on the basis of the results achieved in examinations.

There was a growing number of secondary schools for girls in the city, including the Dominican College for Catholic girls on Eccles Street. Alexandra College, on Earlsfort Terrace, pioneered the education of Protestant girls and sent an increasing number of its pupils on to university.

The city's universities were also significantly divided by religion. Trinity College was founded in 1592 and was, by the mid-nineteenth century, one of the largest and most important universities in the United Kingdom. In 1911, among its renowned fellows and scholars were the classicist Robert Tyrell and the historians

J.P. Mahaffy and J.B. Bury. Many of its students came from England. In 1904 it had begun to admit women students, and it continued to draw students from all across Ireland.

Trinity College was stagnating in terms of numbers attending, however, principally because of religious prohibitions which dissuaded the Catholic middle classes from studying there. The Irish Universities Act of 1908, which created the National University of Ireland, did much to improve the position of one of its constituent colleges, University College Dublin, and gave a massive impetus to Catholic university-level education. Its medical and engineering courses were particularly well thought of.

The college, on St Stephen's Green, was staffed by excellent teachers including Eoin MacNeill, Thomas MacDonagh, George Sigerson and Thomas Kettle, who were all prominent in Irish political life. There was also a number of female staff members, including Agnes O'Farrelly, a lecturer in modern Irish.

In 1911 the Royal College of Science for Ireland moved into its new premises on Upper Merrion Street, which was designed by Aston Webb and Thomas Manly Deane. It offered courses across the sciences, in engineering and in agriculture, with practical laboratory work central to its teaching. Its buildings were later incorporated into UCD, and are now the headquarters of the government. Other educational institutions included the Royal Hibernian Military School and the Drummond Institute in Chapelizod, the Richmond National Institution for the Industrious Blind at Upper Sackville Street, and a horticultural school in Clonturk.

Learning in the city was not, of course, confined to the universities. There was a growing network of libraries, with the National Library on Kildare Street at its core. The Public Libraries Act of 1902 facilitated

the development of smaller libraries across the city. The Royal Irish Academy was a significant place of learning in the capital, promoting research and publications in science, the arts, antiquities and history.

The Royal Hibernian Academy of Arts was in the process of dramatic expansion under its president, Dermod O'Brien, who had assumed office in 1910. The Royal Irish Academy of Music in Westland Row was vital in the provision of music lessons and in holding examinations. In 1911 its director was the influential Michele Esposito who lived at Sandford Road, Ranelagh. ✿

IRISH RAILWAYMEN GO ON STRIKE

ALARMING OUTLOOK

SEQUEL TO DUBLIN TIMBER DISPUTE

SCENES AT DUBLIN TERMINI

This week-end finds Ireland faced with another railway strike, which at present threatens to assume alarming proportions.

For some time past there has been a dispute in the timber trade in Dublin, and about noon on Friday some loads of timber from Messrs. Joseph Kelly and Co., of Thomas street, were taken to Kingsbridge Station to be forwarded to the country. Some of the employees of this timber firm are involved in the dispute, and on this account two of the railwaymen whose duty it was to receive the goods declined to do so.

The two men asked for an interview with the traffic manager, who subsequently saw them and explained that the company were legally bound to accept all goods tendered them for conveyance, and the company could not permit themselves to be put in the position of taking sides in any dispute between city merchants and their employes. He told them the company must insist on the goods being received, and that they should carefully consider their position.

Subsequently the men, having in the meantime consulted with the secretary of the men's Union, decided to go out, and the majority of the goods staff left the premises in a body.

At night affairs assumed more serious proportions, when practically every man of the platform or "coaching" staff joined those who were already out.

Mr. C. Dent, in a reply to a letter from one of the men, stated that, having regard to the company's legal obligations, they could not possibly accede to the condition that the men should decide what traffic they would handle.

Late yesterday it was announced that the men on the Great Northern goods staff had all gone out, and the majority of the men at the goods stores of the Midland Great Western at the North Wall also joined the strikers.

THE ORDINARY MAN'S VIEW OF THE STRIKE EPIDEMIC

SUNDAY INDEPENDENT,
24 SEPTEMBER 1911

PROVISIONS UP.

Provisions are increasing in price, and on Thursday creamery butter could not be got less than 1s. 4½d. per lb. wholesale, while farmers' butter has gone up to 1s. 3d. per lb. wholesale. … It is expected that prices will be further increased. Eggs have gone up to as much as 2s. 6d. per hundred. The poultry industry is considerably disorganised, and no foreign birds are imported at this time of the year. The price of damsons and plums has been almost trebled and that of tomatoes doubled. Hundreds of tons of produce are lying derelict at the railway stations.

IRISH INDEPENDENT,
27 SEPTEMBER 1911

CITY BAKERS' STRIKE

SMALLER FIRMS YIELD

BREAD SUPPLY ENDANGERED

In connection with the bakers' strike in Dublin it was intimated yesterday, at a meeting of employers, held in the Imperial Hotel, that during Monday night the Executive of the men's Society had visited the bakeries of the following firms and instructed the men to stop work:

MESSRS. BOLAND, LTD.; PETER KENNEDY; SIR JOSEPH DOWNES; PATRICK MONKS AND CO.; JAMES KENNEDY, CABINTEELY; JAMES ROURKE; CONNOLLY AND CO., LTD.; WEST CITY BAKERY; DUBLIN BREAD COMPANY, LTD.; AND THE DUBLIN INDUSTRIAL CO-OPERATIVE SOCIETY.

These were the houses represented at the employers' meeting.

The men, active on the instruction, did not go in to work yesterday. A statement in the subjoined terms was issued by the secretary of the employers' meeting:

WE HAVE BEEN REQUESTED BY THE ABOVE BAKERS TO INFORM THE PUBLIC THAT, IN CONSEQUENCE OF THE OPERATIVE BAKERS CARRYING OUT THEIR THREAT TO CEASE WORK ON SIX HOURS' NOTICE, THE FIRMS INVOLVED MUCH REGRET THAT THEY WILL BE UNABLE TO SUPPLY THEIR CUSTOMERS TO-MORROW (WEDNESDAY), AND UNTIL FURTHER NOTICE.

The Great Bread Famine—GOOD NEWS for All!

MEN'S DEMANDS

Mr. Lea, secretary of the men's organisation, stated that 16 or 17 houses were affected, and that replies had been received from six granting their demands. The men, he said, would not go back to any of the houses which had not consented to the terms put forward.

The demands involve, in the case of houses having the time system, a reversion to the result system, as well as increased wages, and, in the case of the houses where the result system is in operation, an increase of wages.

It is stated that the master bakers not affected by the strike have given their word not to increase the supply of bread usually baked. Three-fourths of the bread supply of the city is in the hands of the houses affected.

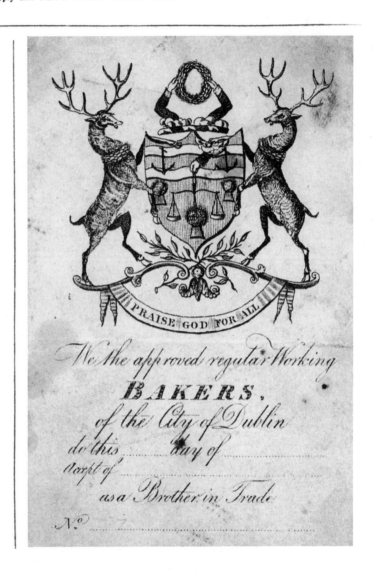

171

Cask cleansing shed, St James's Gate Brewery.

Commerce
& Employment

There was virtually no evidence of economic growth in Dublin in 1911. Many of the traditional industries in the city were struggling to survive, let alone prosper. Work in construction and in the port was inadequate to absorb the surplus labour pool. There were few new firms opening, and no sense of a thriving industrial city. The city was riven with workers' disputes.

Members of the trade union movement were determined to improve the appalling conditions of the working classes, and confrontation with employers was looming. Such was the stagnation in manufacturing that by 1911 the percentage of the workforce employed in that sector was down to 20% from 33% in 1841.

Industry in Dublin, with a few notable exceptions, was geared towards production for the finite home market, and faced challenges from imported goods, although a lot of what was bought in the city was made in the city. There were people making coffins, clocks, cabinets, brushes, mattresses, combs, umbrellas, tobacco pipes and cigarettes. Many of the old trades survived. There were chandlers, ironmongers, sawyers, coopers, bottle blowers, horse-shoers, apothecaries, and all manner of smiths: blacksmiths, whitesmiths, coppersmiths and goldsmiths.

As a reminder that Dublin was an agricultural town as well as a capital city, there were also farm labourers and field workers living in the heart of the city, as well as cow-keepers, cattle-drovers, shepherds, and herdsmen.

In 1911 the textile industry still survived, notably in the Liberties, with almost 200 active looms, but the cotton industry had collapsed and the city had been inundated with cheaply produced English clothes after the 1860s. There were still silk weavers and flax dressers, and all around Greenmount Lane in Rathmines there were numerous linen weavers and winders. Across the city, women sought to supplement their income by making bags, vests, dresses, hats and much else, but individuals were unable to compete with the big mills.

Ship building had all but disappeared from Dublin port until the Dublin Dockyard Company revived it in 1901. There were also companies engaged in the manufacture of matches, chemicals and confectionery, with Jacob's biscuit factory in Bishop Street, for example, employing more than 3,000 people, many of them women.

There were some outstanding employers in the city, notably the Guinness brewery, a company with a long reputation for treating their workforce in a decent manner. With good job security and above-average wages, a job at Guinness was highly prized. Distillers like Jameson's were also major employers. Jobs in the transport sector were coveted. Dublin had traditionally been the centre of the coach-building industry and, by 1910, surviving firms in the city such as Huttons had diversified into motor cars.

Men work in the wash house of the Manor Mill Laundry, Dundrum, Dublin.

Flower sellers on Sackville Street.

A view of Sir Howard Grubb's Optical Works in Rathmines. Here many major telescopes were manufactured for locations around the world. During the lead up to World War I, the works were also used for making gunsights and periscopes for British submarines.

The major transport works in the Inchicore and Phibsborough areas belonging to companies such as the Great Southern and Western Railway Companies and the Dublin United Tramway Company gave valuable employment to skilled and semi-skilled workers, as well as to labourers.

On a smaller scale, there were elements of business life in the city which could claim to be as advanced as, or even ahead of, the rest of the world. Near Observatory Lane at the Rathmines Road there was a remarkable telescope-making factory, owned by Sir Howard Grubb who lived on Orwell Road in Rathgar. The company made telescopes for the Dunsink Observatory and various governments across the world; two telescopes made for the tsarist government in Russia just before the revolution were subsequently paid for by the new Bolshevik government.

Guglielmo Marconi was also engaged in pioneering the use of wireless radio from his base in Dublin. Marconi was born in Italy but his mother was Annie Jameson, from the wealthy Irish whiskey-distilling family. In July 1897, he had transmitted the first ever live report of a sporting event when he commented on a race at the Kingstown regatta from a steamboat in the bay, and he continued to experiment with radio all across Ireland.

There were other areas of innovation, including an artificial leg-maker in Chatham Street, and scientific instrument makers.

Dublin followed changes in other economies with its new class of electricians, electrical engineers and electric lift attendants. Generally, though, Dublin had failed to innovate and had fallen behind Belfast in almost every area of business.

However, Dublin was an important legal, financial and commercial centre, even if it was a provincial one. There was a lucrative trade in selling advertising. The major banks were based in Dublin, as were the Irish headquarters of the large British insurance companies. The city had a substantial stock exchange which had been established by a 1799 bill to regulate the growing number of stockbrokers in the city.

It was a city where many owed their employment to government. As well as departmental officials, there was a growing number of people employed to work as firemen, postmen, labourers and lamplighters.

By 1911 the city's retail trade was changing. The second half of the nineteenth century had seen the arrival of major department stores. Eason's opened in 1886 as a bookseller and newsagent, and Brown Thomas and Clery's were operational. There was criticism in some quarters of the fact that two of the major department stores, McBirney's and Arnott's, were owned by a Scot and an Englishman, respectively. However, the majority of people shopped in small local shops, in the many markets that were scattered across Dublin, or bought from the squadrons of women and children who sold goods on the street. ❧

OCCUPATIONS IN DUBLIN CITY, 1911

	Proportion of workforce				Gender by occupation		
Occupation	Male	Female	Total		Male	Female	Total
Labourer	24.0%	0.3%	11.5%		98.7%	1.3%	19712
Domestic	1.2%	13.5%	7.7%		7.5%	92.5%	12703
Textiles	4.1%	7.5%	5.9%		32.9%	67.1%	9760
Scholar	1.5%	1.8%	1.7%		43.1%	56.9%	2803
Grocer	2.7%	0.5%	1.6%		82.3%	17.7%	2610
Law & Commerce	1.9%	0.2%	1.0%		87.5%	12.5%	1662
Maritime	1.2%	0.7%	0.9%		60.8%	39.2%	1515
Baker	1.4%	0.3%	0.8%		78.6%	21.4%	1420
Nurse	0.0%	1.6%	0.9%		1.4%	98.6%	1412
Military	1.5%	0.1%	0.7%		95.7%	4.3%	1275
Teacher	0.3%	0.9%	0.6%		23.6%	76.4%	1068
Alcohol Industry	1.2%	0.1%	0.6%		92.6%	7.4%	1034
Butcher	1.2%	0.0%	0.6%		96.5%	3.5%	975
Police	1.0%	0.0%	0.5%		98.2%	1.8%	811
Apprentice	0.8%	0.2%	0.5%		82.2%	17.8%	775
Health Professional	0.7%	0.0%	0.3%		95.0%	5.0%	558
Other	50.8%	18.5%	33.8%		71.2%	28.8%	57186
Not Stated	4.6%	53.7%	30.4%		7.1%	92.9%	50523
Totals	100	100	100				167802

Occupations in Dublin city extracted from the census files. Note that occupations are gender-specific and that about 34% of occupations are listed as 'Other'. The data here is based on an analysis of the working population and is confined to those aged fifteen years and older.

S1 M2 T3 W4 T5 F6 S7 ○S8 M9 T10 W11 T12 F13 ◐S14 S15 M16 T17 W18 T19 F20 S21 ● S22 M23 T24 W25 T26 F27 S28 S29 ◗M30 T31

Holidays and Observances

8...Full Moon, 4.11am   12...Old Michaelmas Day   14...Last Quarter 23.46pm   22...New Moon, 4.09am Annular Eclipse of the Sun, invisible throughout the British Isles

30...First Quarter, 6.42am   31...October Bank Holiday, Halloween

Charles Stewart Parnell

PARNELL'S MEMORY

THE STATUE UNVEILED

A GIGANTIC IRISH DEMONSTRATION IN DUBLIN

IMMENSE PROCESSION IN THE STREETS

THREE PROVINCES IN FORCE

In his fascinating autobiography, Sir William Butler says – "I looked upon Parnell as one of the most remarkable men then (1888) living in the Empire. To-day, twenty-two years later, I regard him as the greatest leader of his time." We are now in a position to appraise in a dispassionate spirit the genius, the capacity, and the labour of Parnell.

He found Ireland feeble, despondent, and despairful. Beginning his campaign almost single-handed, he succeeded in a few short years in infusing into the people a national spirit not eclipsed or equalled perhaps, since the days of the Volunteers and Grattan's noble movement. It is unnecessary to recall in all its poignant details the history of Ireland in the years preceding the Parnell movement. ☞

TO PARNELL'S MEMORY

John Redmond at the Parnell monument in 1912. The monument became a rallying point in the city. The traditional poles of the public stands are visible in this image.

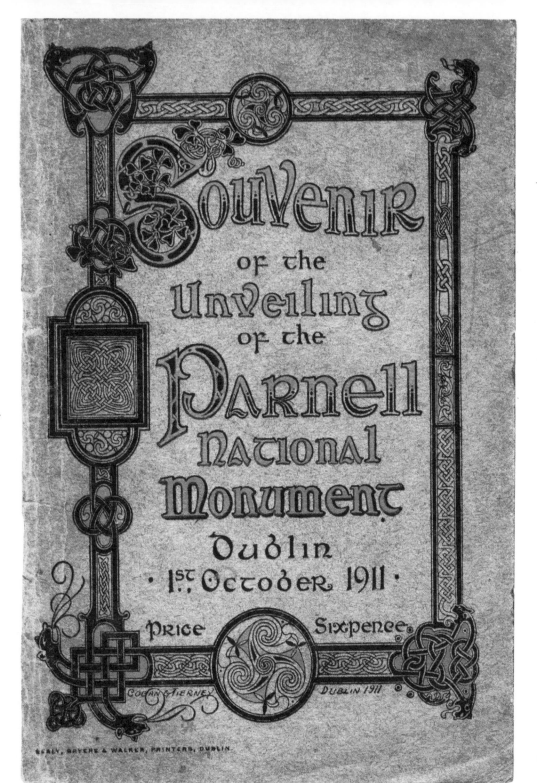

'Souvenir of the Unveiling of the Parnell National Monument. Price sixpence.'

Mr. Redmond, in his warm and eloquent tribute to the memory of the departed leader, gave an epitome of the times which will enable him who has not devoted study to the condition of the country in those days to form a conception of the colossal nature of the task which Parnell undertook and the remarkably brilliant success which the Irish Party under his capable leadership achieved.

Whatever faults the Irish people may have, ingratitude or want of reverence for the memory of the dead who toiled and suffered for the motherland cannot be numbered among them. What more cogent and striking proof of this proposition could be offered than the magnificent and inspiring demonstration which took place yesterday in the metropolis. Despite the untoward circumstances which made it impossible for contingents to come from the South and West, the procession assumed huge proportions. It was fully three miles in length, and it took one hour and forty minutes to pass a given point. Nothing to compare with it has been witnessed in Dublin since 1898. The trades mustered in fine force, whilst among individual counties Wicklow, Parnell's native place, supplied the biggest contingent.

OCT. SUNDAY I.
16th after Trinity.

Unveiling of the Parnell Monument. Went with Columb. Tremendous crowd. Saw John Redmond. Out with Columb to Houston's. Met Miss Alderton and Molly Maguire. Tea there. Brought Columb back to supper

Extract from the diary of Joseph Mary Plunkett.

LEINSTER FOOTBALL CHAMPIONSHIP

KILKENNY, 2-4; MEATH, 1-1

Yesterday, at Jones's road, the Kilkenny footballers defeated Meath in the final of the Leinster Football Championship as above, and thus completed the double event for the Marble County, as their hurlers won the hurling final on Sunday last.

Notwithstanding the threatening nature of the weather, large crowds travelled to the capital with the teams, and there were about four thousand spectators present, the gate receipts totalling close to £100.

The game was advertised for 1.45, and about that hour the Meath team took to the field, few, if any, of the Kilkenny team being on the ground at the time. At about 2.05 Mr J.J. Hogan, Chairman of the Leinster Council, after waiting for the Kilkenny men, who did not come on, awarded Meath the match, and the players retired to the dressingroom.

Some time afterwards, the entire Kilkenny team having arrived, the Royal County representatives were approached, and it was ultimately decided to start the game, Meath playing under protest.

The rain was descending freely when the teams at 2.35 finally took the field, and Mr. M.P. Crowe lost little time in starting the game.

THE TEAMS

MEATH – S. Rennix (goal), J. Newman (capt.), M. Newman, D. Matthews, J. Mallon, M. Ward, J. Shaw, M. Hynes, J. Daly, C. Cummins, P. Wallis, J. Fox, P. Timmins, J. Coogan, W. Donegan, T. Clarke, T. Farrelly.

KILKENNY – R. Holohan, P. Dalton, W. Dalton, R. Dalton, J. Doyle, J. Dwyer, W. Dwyer, J. Donovan, J. Coady, R. Purcell, W. Hoynes, M. Hoynes, J. Fitzgerald, P. Power, W. Sauders, T. Brennan, T. Butler.

THE GAME

Meath broke away on the ball being thrown in, and soon swarmed the Kilkenny posts, a goal being rushed in the first minute. Kilkenny, who had not yet settled down, soon got going, and rushing down the field, the Meath custodian left his charge and the opposing full forward shot an easy goal, amidst loud cheers. After the Kilkenny defence had been unsuccessfully tested, a free against a Meath player enabled Dalton to put his side leading by a point. On resuming, Kilkenny got a free in front of the posts, Dalton scoring a second point. Meath so far were making a plucky fight, and their full forward being fouled when well placed, Newman kicked a minor off the resulting free. A series of frees now took place, Kilkenny getting the better of matters, and after Shaw had saved his side, the Knocktopher boys came with renewed vigour, and Dalton shot a goal. There was no further score before the interval, when Kilkenny led 2-2 to 1-1.

The rain had increased when the teams restarted, leaving the ground in a very bad condition. The Royal County put up a stubborn defence, but they never looked like equalising, and Kilkenny, playing up in surprising style all through, were good winners as above at the final whistle.

A PROTEST

At a meeting of the Leinster Council, held after the game, Mr. J. McNamee gave notice that at the next meeting of the Council he would move that Meath be awarded the match, owing to the fact that Kilkenny failed to line out at the appointed time (1.45), and that Meath played the game under protest.

SPORT NEWSPAPER, SEPTEMBER/ OCTOBER 1911

SATURDAY, 23 SEPTEMBER 1911
The final tie of the Leinster football championship, which was to be played to-morrow at Jones's Road, has been postponed owing to the railway strike.

SATURDAY, 30 SEPTEMBER 1911
The final tie of the Leinster football championship, which was to be played at Jones's Road last Saturday, was not brought off, as the railway companies, owing to the strike, could not run special trains for the conveyance of the teams.

SATURDAY, 14 OCTOBER 1911
The final tie of the Leinster Football Championship will be played at Jones's Road, Dublin, on October 22, between Meath and Kilkenny County teams. Special trains will be run to Dublin on the date of the match – from Waterford at 8.45am, Kilkenny at 10am, Carlow at 10.50, and are due to arrive in Dublin, after calling at all stations, at 12.35. A special train will also be run from Kingscourt at 9am, and is due at Broadstone, after calling at all intermediate stations, at 11.15. A special fast train will also be run from Navan at 10.45.

SATURDAY, 21 OCTOBER 1911
The final tie of the Leinster Senior Football Championship will be played at Jones's Road to-morrow between teams representing Kilkenny and Meath. The fixture was making for September 24th but had to be postponed owing to the railway strike, and since then both sides have been doing all they can in the way of selecting and training so their teams on Sunday may be in the very best form. A close match is expected and the winning team will meet Ulster in the Semi-Final of the All-Ireland Championship.

SATURDAY, 28 OCTOBER 1911
There were several "regrettable incidents" in connection with this match, which was played on Sunday at Jones's road. To be brief, Kilkenny were late in turning up, Meath were awarded a walk-over, Meath refused to accept same, Kilkenny won very decisively, Meath lodged a protest against Kilkenny being declared Leinster Champions, and last, but by no means, least, the match was played in a downpour, which, added to the tedious delay, did not make for the enjoyment of the very large attendance, who travelled from all corners of Leinster to witness the match. The question of Kilkenny's non-attendance, and Meath's subsequent protest was dealt with at a meeting of the Leinster Council held later.

Tom Burke winning a race in Jones's Road.

SPORT

Dublin did not develop professional sporting leagues as did Belfast or the northern industrial cities of Britain, but amateur sport was a vital part of life in the city in 1911. Sport was played by all classes and in all areas, a diverse and increasingly popular phenomenon across Dublin. Conspicuous displays of leisure were an integral part of the lives of wealthy Dubliners; sporting events like hunting, shooting and fishing expeditions were social gatherings as well as competitive endeavours.

The middle classes enjoyed the major elements of the Victorian sporting revolution (in rugby, soccer, tennis and cricket), and games were an integral part of suburban life in schools and clubs. Parts of that sporting revolution were adopted by the working classes. Older traditions also survived. Some blood sports, despite being banned for almost a century, survived in working-class areas where cock fights were a regular feature of life, especially around the Blackpitts in the south city.

Soccer was the most popular sport in Dublin. Having started in the 1880s, it quickly took root in the city. In 1911 there were 31 pitches in use in the Phoenix Park; 29 of them were used for soccer, just two for Gaelic football. Dublin teams, such as Bohemians, played against professional teams from Belfast in the Irish League.

Bohemians FC, based at Dalymount Park, were a proudly amateur outfit, drawn heavily from past pupils of Castleknock College, while Shelbourne Football Club turned professional in 1906 in an attempt to match the northern teams in the Irish League. Their success in winning the Irish cup that year led to huge celebrations in Ringsend and Sandymount, and they did it again in 1911, when victory was ensured by their best player, Val Harris of Erne Street.

If soccer was the most popular contact sport in the city, rugby was the longest established. Rugby in Dublin was the preserve of the prosperous middle classes, and Trinity College had the second oldest rugby club in the country. Among the many famous families who played for the club, the Clinches, Andrew and James, were probably the best known. One of the founders of Bective Rangers Rugby Club, Harvey du Cros, was also an Irish boxing and fencing champion, and was a central force in the promotion of cycle racing in the city, with many races staged in the Phoenix Park. Many important cycling and athletics meetings were held in the fields at Jones' Road, just north of the Royal Canal. The grounds there had also been used for several years to play all-Ireland hurling and football finals, and were owned by Frank Dineen, a journalist. He later sold them to the Gaelic Athletic Association, who renamed the stadium Croke Park in 1913. In 1911 the GAA was struggling to establish itself in the city, despite the fact that its headquarters and its most important stadium were based there. Many of the people who played hurling in the city's clubs were originally from the hurling heartlands of Munster.

The GAA secretary, Luke O'Toole, who served from 1901 to 1929, lived in Mount Pleasant Square, and his house was at one time the official headquarters of the association. The year 1911 saw the donation by George Sigerson, a professor at University College Dublin, of the Sigerson Cup for Gaelic football, played for by the universities of Ireland.

If the GAA was eventually to prosper in Dublin, cricket was moving from being one of the most prominent games in Dublin to a minority interest. Cricket had been played in Dublin since as early as 1792, and in the mid-nineteenth century it was the most popular game in the city. It had, by now, been surpassed by other sports, and cricket became a game largely (though far from exclusively) confined to the wealthier Dublin suburbs.

Sir Stanley Cochrane of Rathmichael, heir to the Cantrell and Cochrane soft-drinks dynasty, owned a private cricket pitch in Woodbrook, south County Dublin. Cochrane built a private railway station at the ground, as well as an indoor cricket school, and employed several English professionals. Cricket clubs were rarely independent ventures and were almost always part of a general suburban sporting club which included hockey, tennis, bowls and much else. ☞

"CONCRETE"
FOOTBALL BOOTS

FOR RUGBY & ASSOCIATION
WEAR.

Golf was also a growing interest for Dubliners. There were courses in play all across Dublin and the first great Irish golfer, Michael Moran, was born on North Great Bull Island. He dominated Irish golf, winning five successive championships from 1909, but besides Moran there were a surprising number of professional golfers, and caddies to tend to them, across Dublin.

Bookmakers were present at virtually every sporting event of note in the city. In some sports there were attempts to ban them but betting survived on the fringes. One of the most popular sports in Dublin in 1911 was billiards. There were billiard halls in many parts of the city, numerous hotels had billiard tables, and quite a number of men found employment as billiard markers.

The Victorian sports revolution and its aftermath are perceived largely as a male affair, but as sports were codified women were involved at various levels. The popularity of tennis, a sport traditionally associated with the wealthier classes, among women, suggests that women's involvement in sport began in the upper classes. Upper- and middle-class women were also involved in hunting and horse-riding, and in hockey, tennis, swimming, camogie clubs and boat clubs.

Agnes O'Farrelly (Úna Ní Fhaircheallaigh), one of the early graduates of the Royal University of Ireland, was a lecturer in modern Irish in UCD from 1909. She later became a professor of modern Irish poetry on the retirement of Douglas Hyde. O'Farrelly founded the UCD camogie club and convinced William Gibson, second Lord Ashbourne, to present a cup, still played for today, to the intervarsity Camogie Championships.

Women also used the many bathing houses which operated in Dublin, with many of the pools having a central wall dividing them into spaces for men and women. There were the Seapoint Baths, the Merrion Pier and Baths on Sandymount Strand, east of the Martello tower, and the Clontarf Baths and Assembly Rooms which were fitted with heated seawater baths.

A remarkably vibrant swimming community existed in 1911. The Irish championships were dominated by the sons of Sir Maurice Dockrell from Monkstown. Henry Morgan Dockrell captained the Irish water polo team and won six Irish titles. George Shannon Dockrell then took over and was recognised as the best swimmer of his generation, winning twenty Irish titles.

Another prominent swimmer was the distinguished doctor, writer and wit, and model for Joyce's Buck Mulligan, Oliver St John Gogarty of Ely Place. Gogarty also played soccer with Bohemians FC and competed regularly in the Irish cycling championships. All-round sportsmen such as Gogarty were a staple of life in Edwardian Dublin. Pride of place must go to George Francis Fitzgerald, a physicist based at Trinity College. Fitzgerald was an outstanding oarsman, a champion pole-vaulter and a hurler. He also tried to fly in 1895 using a winged contraption and a runway against the Pavilion in College Park.

Horse racing was one pursuit which united rich and poor, and had been given an added impetus by the development of the railways in the second half of the nineteenth century. There was a long tradition of race meetings in Dublin, notably in Crumlin, Baldoyle, Fairyhouse and Leopardstown. Across Dublin there were horse trainers and jockeys as well as an entire racing infrastructure. ❀

Spectators at the races.

W1 T2 F3 S4 S5 ○ M6 T7 W8 T9 F10 S11 S12 ◗ M13 T14 W15 T16 F17 S18 S19 ● M20 T21 W22 T23 F24 S25 S26 M27 T28 ◗ W29 T30 F31

Holidays and Observances

6…Full Moon, 3.48pm Penumbral Eclipse of the Moon: the middle of the eclipse occurs at 3.37pm   11…Half-Quarter Day. Martinmas

13…Last Quarter, 7.20am   20…New Moon, 8.49pm   29…First Quarter, 1.42am   30…St. Andrew's Day

IRISH INDEPENDENT,
2 NOVEMBER 1911

DUBLIN AND DISTRICT

City Taxi-Cab Service

The Dublin Motor Car Co. yesterday inaugurated a taxi cab service in the city with a trip for five passengers, at a fare of half-a-crown, from Parliament street, via O'Connell street and North Circular road, to Phoenix Park, returning by the quays. Those, including jarveys, who noted the innovation, watched the progress of the taxi – an Austin landaulette, with taximeter and "red flag" to attract intending customers – with much curiosity. The cars have the full D.M.P. licence, except for standing at the hazards, and the tariff is 10d. per mile, with a minimum of 2s. 6d., which covers three miles, and there are no extras. Above 2s. 6d., the charge is 2d. per fifth of a mile.

CITY
TRANSPORT

In 1911 Dublin was served by an impressive public transport system, and was also beginning to cater for the demands of the city's increasing number of private motorists. As well as its internal transport network, Dublin was the focal point of the national system, a vital hub in the commercial and social life of the country.

The iconic means of public transport of the time was the Dublin tram. The electrified trams of 1911 had replaced the original horse-drawn trams, which in turn had replaced the horse-drawn omnibus. There were, by 1911, 330 trams operating on lines which ran for 60 miles along the city's roads, drawing the suburbs tightly to the city. Dubliners believed that many of the people who came to work for the tram companies were from the country. In his book *Dublin made me*, C.S. Andrews (b. 1901) claimed that the Dublin United Tram Company had a policy of recruiting non-Dubliners. In part this was because the original trams were horse-drawn and reflected the ability of country people to work with horses. But the trend was thought to have continued, and many of the tram drivers and conductors living in the suburb of Terenure were originally from County Westmeath.

People working for the rail companies also tended to cluster in certain areas. There were numerous examples of this, including

The three main kinds of transport on view: tram, bicycle and horse and cart on the corner of Grafton Street and Nassau Street.

Great Western Square off the North Circular Road, which was occupied by employees of the Midland Great Western Railway. The numerous jobs associated with the railways ensured that people who worked for them had a presence all over the city, and there were also many people who lived on the dividends from railway shares.

The first railway line in Ireland had opened on 17 December 1834, when the Dublin city centre station of Westland Row was linked to the port of Kingstown. The railways were important to the development of suburban Dublin in their facilitation of commuters travelling to work in the city centre. By the end of the First World War there were over 3,500 miles of railway in Ireland, with Dublin the focal point of the network. The popularity of the links from Dublin is demonstrated by the addition of a second storey to Kingsbridge station in 1911.

A mutually beneficial leisure industry was developed in tandem with the railways. The expanding middle class adopted a culture of day-tripping which benefited Dublin coastal villages such as Blackrock and Kingstown. Seaside resorts grew and race meetings were established, along with a host of other sporting events such as regattas and galas.

The importance of the railways extended even to the notion of time in the city. The development of railway timetables was critical to the passing of the Time Act in 1880, establishing Dublin Mean Time across Ireland. Previously, clocks in Cork were eleven minutes behind those of Dublin, while those in Belfast were one minute and nineteen seconds ahead. In 1911 Dublin was still 25 minutes behind London, and it was only in 1916 that Greenwich Mean Time was extended to Ireland.

Ireland had been to the forefront of the cycling craze which swept the western world in the late-Victorian era. It wasn't merely that the Irish adopted the 👉

The Cars on the Several Routes are distinguished, in addition to the Name Boards on each side and the Destination Indicators at either end, by the Following Signs above the destination Indicators:—

Route	Sign	Route	Sign
NELSON'S PILLAR AND TERENURE (VIA RATHMINES)		RATHFARNHAM AND DRUMCONDRA (VIA HAROLD'S CROSS)	
NELSON'S PILLAR AND DARTRY ROAD (VIA UPPER RATHMINES)		RIALTO AND GLASNEVIN (VIA DOLPHIN'S BARN)	
DONNYBROOK AND PHŒNIX PARK (VIA MERRION SQUARE)		NELSON'S PILLAR AND DALKEY	
DONNYBROOK AND PHŒNIX PARK (VIA STEPHEN'S GREEN)		NELSON'S PILLAR AND CLONSKEA (VIA LEESON STREET)	
KINGSBRIDGE AND HATCH STREET (VIA SOUTHERN QUAYS & WESTLAND ROW)		NELSON'S PILLAR & SANDYMOUNT (VIA RINGSEND)	
PARK GATE AND BALLYBOUGH		NELSON'S PILLAR & DOLLYMOUNT	
INCHICORE AND WESTLAND ROW		COLLEGE GREEN & WHITEHALL (VIA CAPEL ST. & DRUMCONDRA)	
O'CONNELL BRIDGE & PARK GATE (VIA NORTHERN QUAYS)		KENILWORTH ROAD AND LANSDOWNE ROAD	
NELSON'S PILLAR & PALMERSTON PARK			

The trams in Dublin all used a symbol rather than a number, ensuring that even those who were not numerically literate could know that the shamrock meant the 'Nelson's Pillar/Dalkey' line, or if you caught the red triangle it would take you to Terenure.

bicycle; they also contributed to its development. John Boyd Dunlop invented the pneumatic tyre in the 1880s after his son had complained of the pain caused by cycling on solid wheels over cobblestones. The tyre was an immediate success and Dunlop went into business with Harvey du Cros, a paper manufacturer of Huguenot origin, manufacturing the tyres at Stephen's Street in Dublin. All across the capital, the tyres were fitted on the growing number of bicycles seen along the city's streets.

Like all other modes of transport, the bicycle came under pressure following the arrival of the motor car. The relentless twentieth-century rise

Motor car, St Stephens Green.

of the private car in Dublin had already begun in 1911. In that year there was a total of 5,058 registered cars, buses and lorries in Ireland, a large proportion of them based in Dublin. Various coachbuilders had adapted their manufacturing plants to build car bodies.

The first petrol car seen in Ireland was owned by a Dubliner, Dr John Colohan, who imported a Benz Velo in 1896.

He was quickly followed by other prominent Dublin citizens such as J.M. Gillies, manager of the *Freeman's Journal*, and Lord Iveagh. When the Royal Irish Automobile Club was founded in 1901, the majority of its members were titled landowners, military officers, or wealthy brewers and distillers. Another car owner was Richard J. Mecredy, a leading cyclist and athlete, who established a newspaper called *Motor News*.

In time the roads of the city facilitated the further development of the bus as a means of public transport but, in 1911, the old usage of the jaunting car remained prominent. Four passengers sat back-to-back, two on each side, as the horse-drawn carriage moved through the streets. This mode of transport survived well into the twentieth century, tradition and modernity living side-by-side. ✾

F1 S2 S3 M4 T5 ○ W6 T7 F8 S9 S10 M11 ☽ T12 W13 T14 F15 S16 S17 M18 T19 ● W20 T21 F22 S23 S24 M25 T26 W27 ☾ T28 F29 S30 S31

Holidays and Observances

3…Advent Sunday   6…Full Moon, 2.52am   12…Last Quarter, 5.46pm   20…New moon, 3.40pm

22…Shortest Day. Winter commences, 10.54pm   25…Christmas Day   26…Bank Holiday   31…Childermas

SOME OPINIONS OF LEADING IRISH PROTESTANTS

At every bye-election in Great Britain an army of speakers and canvassers, paid by the day on a generous scale, is imported from Ulster, and is employed on the ignoble work of slandering their own countrymen and of painting lurid pictures of the intolerance which Protestants are likely to experience under Home Rule at the hands of a Catholic majority.

Henry Grattan said it was "impossible to argue with a prophet—one could only refuse to believe him"; and the vagueness of this particular prediction makes its refutation all the more difficult. It seemed to me, however, that the most effective method of reply would be to invite leading and representative non-Catholics in all parts of Ireland to state their views; and the replies to a circular letter are embodied in the following pages.

MR RICHARD M. BARRINGTON, J.P., M.A., LL.B. (ONE OF THE LARGEST EMPLOYERS OF AGRICULTURAL LABOUR IN THE COUNTY OF WICKLOW).
I have no fear of religious intolerance under Home Rule; and have every confidence in the good sense of my Catholic neighbours and fellow-countrymen.
Fassaroe, Bray

PROFESSOR CROFTON
(Professor of Pathology in the National University of Ireland)
I have never noticed the slightest sign of religious intolerance on the part of Roman Catholics in Ireland—very much the contrary, in fact.

I have spent all my College and University days amongst Catholics, and have never received anything but the greatest kindness and consideration from both professors and students: and now that I am one of the staff of University College my experience is just the same—invariable kindness and consideration, and readiness to help me in every way.

I hope my colleagues hold me in as much esteem and affection as I do them.
National University Dublin

MR. MILES RICHARD HOPKINS
(MANUFACTURING SILVERSMITH AND JEWELLER.)
I never heard in the county in which I was born (County Carlow) any such thing as ill-feeling or persecution by Catholics of any kind whatsoever. On the contrary, wherever my relations and friends had the education and judgement, they got positions of emolument and trust in the country, although the population was, and still is, practically all Catholic.
O'Connell Street, Dublin.

GOVERNMENT & POLITICS

In a city so divided by wealth, class and religion, it was inevitable that politics in Dublin in 1911 were intense, lively, bitter and absorbing. From the debates conducted at public meetings and in council chambers, to the raw conflict of street demonstrations, there was a vibrancy and urgency to political life. The major cataclysms of the 1913 Lockout, the First World War and the 1916 Rising were all to come, and the city was to be deeply affected by all those events. In 1911 nobody could predict the events of the following decade, but many of the principal players were already in place. ☞

No. II.---THE COLOSSUS OF DUBLIN.

Ratepayer (to his Son)---This, my boy, is the Dublin Colossus, made of ratepayers' gold (sometimes called the Doublin' Colossus). This enormous figure, like its relative at Rhodes, which fell into the sea, is preparing for a big dive. Its supports, you see, cannot last for ever.

ENGLISH ADMINISTRATION IN IRELAND

The shameless extravagance and wasteful expenditure which characterise Dublin Castle government may be illustrated in a concise fashion by the following figures. In 1841 the population of Ireland was 8,175,124, and its civil government charges were about £4,000,000. In 1910 the population of Ireland was about 4,000,000, the civil government charges were £9,077,500. The following comparison with Scotland, a country whose population is larger than Ireland's by more than half a million is also eloquent:

Number of Government officials
having more than £160 a year
SCOTLAND/944   IRELAND/4,397

Amount of their salaries:
SCOTLAND/£319,237   IRELAND/£1,441,131

Figures taken from the Inland Revenue Report for 1909–10.

The newest Irish Department is the Department of Agriculture and Technical Instruction. Surely we shall find Catholics getting fair play there? The facts are the reverse. The five principal officials draw salaries to the tune of £5,000 a year. One is a Catholic. The appointment of this one Catholic created more commotion amongst the intolerant minority than any recent episode of Irish departmental history. The man who made the appointment was driven out of public life.

In 1911 primary political power in the country lay with the administration in Dublin Castle. Government was centralised and interventionist. Formal responsibility for the administration of Ireland fell to the lord lieutenant, the earl of Aberdeen, who lived in the vice-regal lodge in the Phoenix Park. He was supported by the chief secretary's office, which was charged with the business of running the country, with a growing body of officials. The chief secretary in 1911 was Augustine Birrell.

By 1911, 3,526 people were employed in central and local government, a tenfold increase from 1841, with the majority based in Dublin. From 1871, recruitment to the civil service was by open competition through examination, and by 1911 an increasing number of civil servants were Catholics.

Following the Act of Union in 1800, Dublin was a city without a parliament, its elected representatives travelling to the House of Commons in London for debates. High politics invariably focused

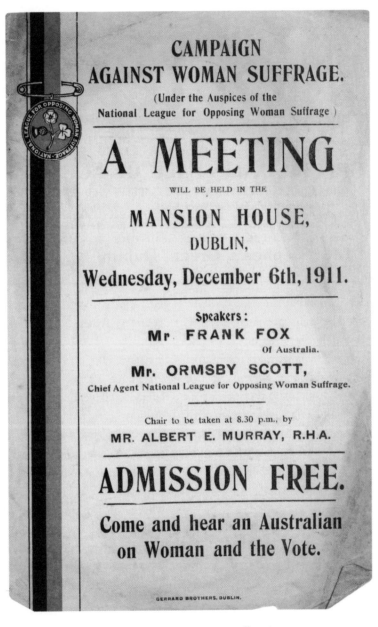

'Campaign against woman suffrage'.

on the national question. In 1911 Dublin was represented by both unionists and nationalists. The city's best-known representative was John Dillon, a key member of the Nationalist Party, whose immediate objective was to win Home Rule for Ireland. Dillon was a brilliant orator who lived in Dublin as a widower raising six children.

Also based in the city was another nationalist, a former MP, Thomas Kettle, married to Mary Sheehy, sister of Hanna Sheehy Skeffington. Kettle was Professor of National Economics at University College Dublin. He had been in Belgium buying guns for the Irish volunteers when the Germans invaded, and was so appalled by the invasion that he subsequently joined the British army. He was later killed in action in France.

The majority of the Dublin electorate was nationalist, but the city still returned unionist MPs, principally through Trinity College, where Sir Edward Carson, the unionist leader, was one of two serving MPs. Indeed, the last unionist to be elected as an MP in Dublin outside of Trinity College was Sir Maurice Dockrell, who was elected for Dublin County in 1918.

A series of reform acts through the nineteenth century reshaped constituencies and broadened the franchise for general elections, to the point where 700,000 Irishmen had the right to vote. By the end of the 1890s, women had successfully campaigned for the right to participate in local elections in Ireland, and a vanguard of Irishwomen continued to fight for their right to vote in parliamentary elections. Working-class women were involved, but the majority of the activists were either white-collar workers, professionals, or married to professionals.

Throughout the nineteenth century local elections provided the platform for a range of gains made by nationalists. In 1841 Daniel O'Connell was elected the city's first Catholic lord mayor since the reformation. The 1880s brought nationalists victories in local elections as part of a revolution in municipal government. By 1911 the greatest proportion of nationalist representatives on Dublin Corporation were small businessmen such as publicans, drapers and grocers.

The Corporation was not successful in addressing the great social problems which lay at the heart of city life. Some progress was made, not least in drainage, sewerage systems, water supply and the provision of electricity and street lighting, but the Corporation was badly hampered by lack of funds. More critically, there was no sense that the Corporation was capable of devising a policy to improve the lives of its most underprivileged inhabitants, not least because fourteen of its members actually owned tenements.

It was against this backdrop that socialist politicians were attempting to organise trade unions and political parties. At their head were James Connolly and James Larkin. In 1910 Connolly published his seminal *Labour in Irish history* and also became the chief organiser of the Socialist Party of Ireland. In 1912, with persuasion from Larkin, the Irish Trade Union Congress voted to establish the Irish Labour Party.

Within five years Connolly and his Irish Citizen Army—of which playwright Seán O'Casey, a working-class Protestant who lived in East Wall, was a member—had joined with radical nationalists in the city to mount an armed insurrection. In 1911 these nationalists were very much in the shadow of their more moderate contemporaries. Though limited in numbers, their presence in the city was still considerable. Arthur Griffith had founded Sinn Féin in 1905 and attracted radical nationalists of many hues, then operating on the fringes of Dublin life.

Thomas Clarke had been back in Ireland since 1907, following fifteen years in English prisons, and was determined to re-establish the Irish Revolutionary Brotherhood as a potent force in the politics of the city. William Cosgrave, future president of the Executive Council of the Irish Free State, and Éamon de Valera, future taoiseach and president, both lived in Dublin in 1911.

Also living in the city were prominent educationalists who were involved in the separatist movement. Eoin McNeill and Thomas MacDonagh were working in University College Dublin, and Pádraig Pearse had established the bilingual St Enda's. Their progress could be seen through the number of people who filled out the census form through Irish. Generally, this was done by members of the Gaelic League, especially teachers. ✳

ARCADIA, THE FAIRIES' PARADISE.

SWITZER'S GRAND CHRISTMAS BAZAAR, DUBLIN

'Let's go to Arcadia,' is the seasonable invitation that greets one everywhere in Dublin, and, trooping to that Mecca of mystery, dear to the heart of the little ones, come day after day, in rapidly increasing number the 'children of a larger growth' intent on evincing in a practical manner their appreciation of the year-end carnival provided for the younger generation by Messrs. Switzer and Co., Ltd., who, during the past decade, have gone 'one better' each year than its predecessor. No more fitting nomencalture than that chosen for the present display could be devised. The name, signifying all that is expressive of song, felicity, innocence and peace, is in itself an attraction, and a descriptive account of the 'Fairies' Paradise' conveys but a faint idea of the reality, which must be seen to be fully appreciated.

This is the impression created in my mind, writes our correspondent, and, putting aside the word pictures drawn by imaginative youth, I determined to see for myself the abode of 'pastoral poetry' brought, so to speak, to our very doors by Messrs. Switzer and Co., of Grafton St. Entering the magic portals of Arcadia I am greeted by a babel of fresh young voices expressive of various stages of delight. Long drawn out 'Oh's!' cries of 'Look at Jumbo, mamma!' 'See the dear little puss in boots!' 'O—h, the lovely swans!' Working my way gently through the crowds of visitors of all ages I come to what may be called something entirely new in Dublin, if, indeed, not in the United Kingdom, in the shape of the Fairies' Paradise. Five swans swim gracefully on a limpid stream of running water, and attached to each is a delightful argosy of valuable toys and other pretty articles. Each swan is driven by a fairy queen, the latter beautifully dressed and crowned with garlands of roses, the guiding reins being of broad silk ribbon of different shade and colour. The realistic effects are enhanced by a cascade of real water trickling from miniature grottos, the surroundings composed of woodlands and mountain scenery, while brilliantly plumed birds of paradise, peacocks, and storks add to the charming tableau. In front of the 'Wonderland' stands a 'little boy blue,' who ever and anon invites the visitors to avail of the chance of procuring some of the ☞

Arcadia at Switzer's
NOW OPEN
Grand   Christmas   Bazaar.

The large set piece represents Arcadia, the Fairies' Paradise. Real Waterfall, Running Streams, Presents conveyed by Swans on Real Water.

Jumbo (the huge Elephant),
Puss in Boots, Candy Floss, &c., &c.

Thousands of Toys for all Ages.

Special Heating and Ventilation.

☞ Admission to Bazaar 2d., which will be allowed on the Purchase of Goods or on Side Shows. Special Reductions made on Toys for Charitable Distribution, Regimental Christmas Trees, &c.

Switzer & Co., Ltd., Grafton Street.

☞ thousands of presents brought from Arcadia by the swans, and few there are that do not respond to the invitation—to buy a 6d. ticket at the adjoining booth and exchange it for a souvenir of the 'Fairies' Paradise.' An enchanting exhibition brilliantly illuminated, the abode of Pan is an outstanding feature of Messrs. Switzer's Grand Christmas Bazaar in Grafton street. Not less exciting to the tiny onlookers and equally interesting to the more matured visitors is 'Jumbo,' the huge elephant, that roars a welcome to his friends and distributes presents with his trunk. A dear little 'Father Christmas,' attired in a scarlet robe, with snow-white locks and long beard to correspond, acts as 'Jumbo's' keeper, and appreciative attention is divided between 'man and beast,' the former suggestive of the happy season of Yuletide, and the latter replete with associations of the Zoo.

Nollaig 1911

This card uses the decorative Irish lettering and spelling which was phased out over the century. In late 1910 the Society for the Simplification of Irish was inaugurated with a lecture. Scholar Osborn Bergin dismissed the objections raised to simplification, one of which ran as follows:

'Objection 3—"The people of Ireland are devoted to the old spelling.";

In a sense I could wish this were true. Unfortunately the people of Ireland, as any publisher of Gaelic books will tell you, care precious little about the old spelling. If they are so devoted to it, why has the *Gaelic Journal* been allowed to die? Why could not a great organisation like the Gaelic League find support for a small monthly organ? Outside the schools and classes, and apart from the various examination programmes, is there any reading public, any demand for books in Irish, which would pay the expense of publication? You know there is not. Those who profess to speak on behalf of "the people of Ireland" and their "national sentiment", are either unable or unwilling to face the facts.'

A Christmas card from Conradh na Gaeilge to those overseas (thar sáile), December 1911.

VOLUMES OF GOOD WISHES

A merry CHRISTMAS

IRISH TIMES,
26 DECEMBER 1911

SWImmING

HALF MOON BATHERS' CLUB

The following, under the leadership of the veteran, McEvoy, took the water on Christmas Day—Messers. Byrne, Booth, Farrell, Gardner, G. Gardner, II, Ironmonger, Knott, Morgan, J. Morgan, P. Moffett, Manning, Patterson, Lewis, and Walsh.

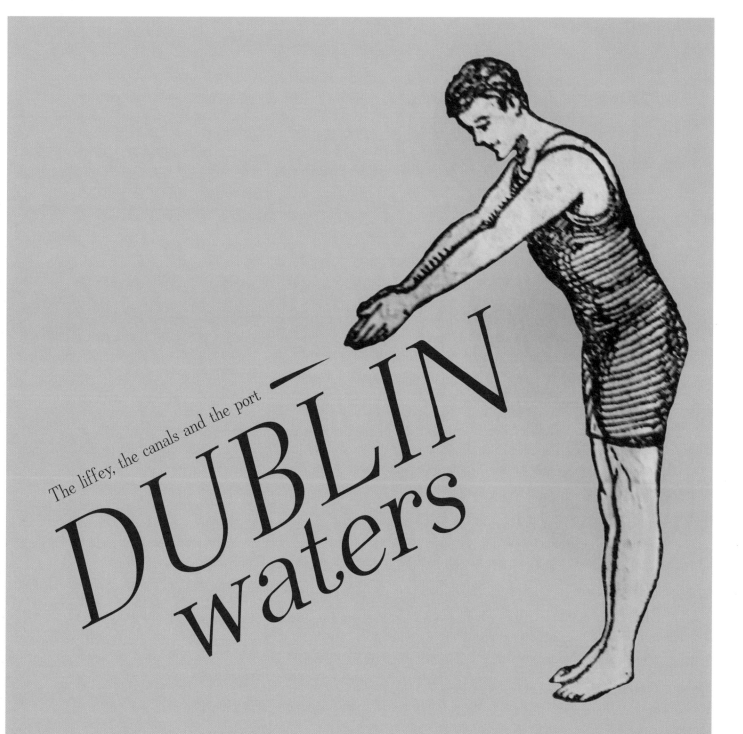

The liffey, the canals and the port

DUBLIN
waters

The River Liffey and its estuary drew the first settlers to build the communities which became Dublin. In 1911, more than a millennium later, the water that flowed through and around the city continued to have a huge impact on the life of its inhabitants. By 1911 all the quays of the Liffey, stretching from Kingsbridge Station (now Heuston Station) to the port had been laid out, and the older ones had been renovated in the preceding decades. The building of the quays was a formidable feat of engineering, and critical to the preservation of bank-side land from the periodic flooding which had blighted its development.

Along the quays were some of the landmark buildings of Dublin, including the Custom House and the Four Courts, both designed by James Gandon. Other buildings were not as architecturally important, but were connected with sea and river life. There were dedicated homes for sailors as well as seaman's institutes. Also on the quays was Moira House which was built in 1752 by Sir John Rawdon. In 1911 the house was being used as a hostel by the Association for the Suppression of Mendicancy in Dublin, to alleviate street begging.

The last of the quays to be completed was Victoria Quay, which was named after Queen Victoria in 1863 when she opened the bridge which joined it and Albert Quay (now known as Wolfe Tone Quay). There was a large community of casual dockers living in the streets near the port. And there were the lively pubs on the quays, where dockers were traditionally paid by the stevedores who controlled their employment.

The Liffey was a vital source of water for the city dwellers, though piped water came from the Vartry River and reservoir at Roundstone. The river was also a much-used dumping ground for sewage and for the city drainage system. In 1906 the first major drainage system was completed; sewers which had previously discharged crude sewage into the Liffey were now intercepted, and their content brought in pipes laid along the quays to a treatment works at the Pigeon House on the south bank of the port.

Crossing the Liffey was often an expensive business. In the early twentieth century some of the bridges were tolled. In 1911 Wellington Bridge still had turnstiles, which were not removed until 1919 when the bridge was opened free to the public. Its toll endured in the public consciousness, and it has retained its popular name: the Ha'penny Bridge. Those who did not cross by bridge often used the ferries which plied their trade downstream from the main retail areas of the city. Through the late nineteenth century there were complaints that the boats, which were generally rowed across, were overcrowded, carrying more than thirty people. By 1911, all five ferry crossings which survived were driven by motors; they were a vital link for communities and businesses at the port end of the Liffey.

Other rivers were enjoyed by Dubliners as places to fish, to walk alongside, or as iconic names in song and verse. The second largest river in the city is the Tolka, which rolled through the agricultural lands to the west of the city, passing through Cabra, Glasnevin, Drumcondra and Ballybough before entering the Irish Sea at the East Wall and Clontarf. The Dodder flowed from the northern slopes of Kippure in the Wicklow Mountains, before winding its way over some 20 kilometres through Tallaght, Rathfarnham, Clonskeagh, Donnybrook, and Ballsbridge, entering the Liffey at Ringsend.

CUSTOM HOUSE DUBLIN. 710 W.L.

For many years, the Poddle provided drinking water for Dublin. Rising in Fettercairn, near Tallaght, it ran through the outlying village of Templeogue and then through the heart of the old city. In 1911 it crossed underground through Dublin Castle, from the Ship Street gate to the Chapel Royal, and then northwards to the Undercroft. It flowed into the Liffey at Wood Quay.

The port itself was critical to the economy of the city. It did not industrialise as intensively as the ports of Belfast, Liverpool or Glasgow and, in 1911, only had a very small-scale shipping industry run by the Dublin Dockyard Company. Sail-makers, marine stores and numerous maritime trades grew around the port. There was also a traditional glass-making industry in the Ringsend area, and sundry other manufacturing concerns around the port. If the port was limited in terms of manufacturing industry, it was,

nonetheless, an absolutely vital trading post for the city and its hinterland.

The trade in imported and exported goods was critical in providing employment for the working-class areas of Ringsend, Irishtown and the North Wall. There were sea captains, carters, crane drivers, shipwrights, marine engineers and fish merchants living in these districts.

In every trade there were many struggling to find work. As the nineteenth century progressed, increasing quantities of British-manufactured goods made their way through the port, as did large shipments of coal. Dublin's position as the focal point of the rail network confirmed the importance of the port as a point of import.

However, Ireland was unable to export much by way of manufactured produce, with the notable exception of Guinness, Jacob's biscuits and a small number of other sought-after items. The bulk of Irish exports were agricultural, and every day shipments of cattle left Dublin port for English farms and slaughterhouses. From the 1870s onwards, seven shipments per day left for British ports, with

even more sailing between September and March.

Emigrants left from the north wall and from the south of the city, where the Dublin Steam Packet Company operated the Kingstown to Holyhead mail and passenger route. For many leaving Ireland, their last sight of land was the lighthouses along the coast. These were the responsibility of the Commissioners of Irish Lights from 1867, and among the permanently manned lighthouses on the Dublin coastline were the Poolbeg Lighthouse and the Baily Lighthouse at Howth. Lighthouses were critical to those who made their living from the sea, not least the many fishermen who fished the waters of Dublin bay.

There were fishing communities all along the coast of north County Dublin. Communities such as Loughshinny depended on the earnings of such fishermen, as well as being home to the coastguards who patrolled the waters. The Royal Navy, too, had a significant presence in Dublin bay. Howth and other Dublin coastal villages such as Clontarf, Blackrock and Kingstown were also renowned as seaside resorts for those with money to spend on leisure. Kingstown, for example, was fashionable for its yachting and other maritime activities, including swimming at the Forty Foot.

As well as yachts and other pleasure boats, there were many rowing boats listed in the census as pleasure crafts moored in the harbour. All along the coast, north and south of the city, small villages prospered from the growth in local tourism and leisure outings. The River Liffey was also a focal point for fishing, rowing clubs and swimming. It, too, developed its own recreational importance, and in 1910 a new hotel and sanatorium was opened on its banks by the Lucan Hydropathic Spa company.

Hotels, built on their banks, had made a significant contribution to the development of the canals which left Dublin. The Royal Canal ran from Dublin to Mullingar, with offshoots running to the Shannon at Cloondara and to Longford. The project became bankrupt before its completion around 1817, and the Royal Canal never proved as profitable as the Grand Canal, which linked Dublin to Shannon Harbour in 1805.

As well as a string of hotels, the canals facilitated the development of breweries, distilleries and other industries. Initially, canals provided for more efficient transport of goods and passengers than existing modes of transport did, but by 1911 they had been largely surpassed by road and rail. The canals remained a focal point of the city and were seen to mark the boundaries of inner-city Dublin.❀

Sailors standing near the seafront in Kingstown.

REFERENCES

PAGE

ii   Chromolithograph from the Paris fashion house of Atelier Bachwitz. Fashionable toque hat made of lime-green glossy straw. Brim is rolled up, crown heightened towards the back. Wide band of narrow feather ruches in the same shade sewn on stiff tulle, same coloured ostrich couteaux at the left (1911).

vi   Cartoon: 'The passing of the barber…perhaps'. *Sunday Independent*, 7 May 1911, 1.

viii   Postcard of O'Connell bridge and Sackville Street. Reverse postmarked August 1911.

JANUARY

1   Notable dates reproduced for this month and all months from Sutton Seeds Catalogue 'My garden diary for 1911'.

2–3   '1911: all New Year joys be yours'. Courtesy of CardCow Vintage Postcards (ref: 189414).

4   Advertisement: 'Clery's Winter sale'. *Irish Times*, 2 January 1911, 2.

5   'Flashes from the footlights'. *Sunday Independent*, 1 January 1911, 4.

7   Postcard: '1911: A Happy New Year'. Courtesy of Far Far Hill Vintage Scans (www.farfarhill.blogspot.com).

9   '1911 Diaries: Hely's, Limited'. *Irish Times*, 3 January 1911, 1.

11   Advertisement: 'Fitzgerald & Co.—Dublin' (1911). Courtesy of the Advertising Archives (ref: 30566240).

12   Advertisement: 'Always ask for Flower & McDonald's Irish Salt' (Programme of Irish language procession; Clár móir-shiubhail na nGaedheal, 18 September 1910, Demonstration Committee, Gaelic League, Dublin, 1910). Courtesy of the Royal Irish Academy Library (ref: RRG/25/G/Box 2/10).

15   Dublin Metropolitan Police constable, O'Connell Street (*c.* 1910). Copyright of the Garda Museum.

17   'Deeds that won the empire: the capture of the poles' (1911). Courtesy of the National Library of Ireland (ref: POL/1910–1920/29).

19   Postcard from James Joyce to Stanislaus Joyce (22 January 1911). Reproduced with kind permission from the James Joyce Estate. Courtesy of the Division of Rare and Manuscript Collections, University of Cornell (ref: 4609/III/Box 5).

20   *Bean na h-Éireann* title banner. Courtesy of the National Library of Ireland.

20   Advertisement: 'Commonwealth of Australia: opportunities for emigrants'. *Irish Times*, 12 January 1911, 3.

21   Mail boat, Kingstown Harbour, Dublin (1880–1914). Courtesy of the National Library of Ireland (ref: LCAB/7246).

FEBRUARY

MARCH

APRIL

MAY

JUNE

JULY

AUGUST

SEPTEMBER

OCTOBER

NOVEMBER

DECEMBER

ALBIO
MILK
AN
SU

PURE
AND
PLEASANT

DELICATE

N LUXURY
IN THE
BATH

D
LPHUR
SOAP
PERFUME.

BIBLIOGRAPHY

BIBLIOGRAPHIC NOTE

The essays in this book are rooted in the census returns for 1911 which, house-by-house, street-by-street, offer a fascinating insight into the life of Dublin in 1911. See: www.census.nationalarchives.ie.

Further information for the essays was taken from the newspapers published in Dublin in 1911, particularly the *Freeman's Journal*, the *Irish Times*, the *Irish Independent* and the *Dublin Evening Mail*. Similarly, the *Dublin Historical Record* journal since 1938 contains a wonderful body of material on the history of the city. Newspaper articles can be browsed at www.irishnewsarchive.com or by visiting the National Library of Ireland and other public libraries and using the microfilm collections. A large number of Irish periodicals are available on JSTOR. Browse the Ireland Collection at: http://about.jstor.org/content-collections/journals/ireland. See also the Dictionary of Irish Biography online at: www.dib.ie.

REPORTS

The census of Ireland for the year 1911. National Library of Ireland (ref: IR 310 c1).
Report of the inter-departmental committee on the employment of children during school-age, especially in street-trading in the large centres of population in Ireland (1902). National Library of Ireland (ref: IR 3313 s5).
Royal Commission on the Poor Law. Report on Ireland (1909). National Library of Ireland (ref: IR 3529 p1).
Report of the Dublin Disturbances Commission (1914). National Library of Ireland (ref: IR 33189 d3).
Report of the departmental committee appointed by the local government board for Ireland to enquire into the housing conditions of the working classes in the city of Dublin (1914). British Parliamentary Papers, vol. 19 (ref: cd. 7272/7317-xix).

BOOKS

Aalen, F.H.A. and Whelan, K. (eds) 1992 *Dublin city and county: from prehistory to present. Studies in honour of J.H. Andrews.* Dublin. Geography Publications.
Andrews, C.S. 1979 *Dublin made me.* Dublin. Mercier Press.
Ball, F. E. 1895 *The parish of Taney: a history of Dundrum, near Dublin, and its neighbourhood.* Dublin. Hodges, Figgis, & Co., Ltd.
Bennett, Douglas 2005 *The encyclopedia of Dublin.* Dublin. Gill & Macmillan.
Boran, Pat 1963 *A short history of Dublin.* Dublin. Mercier Press.

Casey, Christine 2005 *Dublin: the city within the Grand and Royal Canals and the Circular Road with the Phoenix Park*. New Haven, Conn.; London. Yale University Press.

Chart, David 1907 *The story of Dublin*. London. Dent.

Clarke, Howard B. 1978 *Dublin c. 840–c. 1540: the medieval town in the modern city*. Dublin. The Friends of Medieval Dublin.

Connolly, S.J. 1998 *The Oxford companion to Irish history*. Oxford. Oxford University Press.

Conroy, J.C. 1928 *A history of the railways in Ireland*. London, New York. Longmans, Green & Co. Ltd.

Cosgrave, Dillon 1909 *North Dublin: city and environs*. Dublin. Catholic Truth Society of Ireland.

Cosgrove, Art 1988 *Dublin through the ages*. Dublin. College Press.

Cousins, James and Margaret 1950 *We two together*. Madras. Ganesh.

Craig, Maurice James 1969 *Dublin 1660–1860: a social and architectual history*. Dublin. Allen Figgis.

Cullen Owens, Rosemary 1984 *Smashing times: a history of the Irish women's suffrage movement 1889–1922*. Dublin. Attic Press.

Daiken, Leslie 1963 *Out goes she: Dublin street rhymes*. Dublin. The Dolmen Press.

Daly, Mary E. 1984 *Dublin: the deposed capital 1860–1914*. Cork. Cork University Press.

De Courcy, J.W. 1996 *The Liffey in Dublin*. Dublin. Gill & Macmillan.

Dickinson, Page 1926 *The Dublin of yesterday*. London. Methuen & Co., Ltd.

Ellmann, Richard 1986 *Four Dubliners: Wilde, Yeats, Joyce, and Beckett*. Washington. Library of Congress.

Farmar, Tony 2010 *Privileged lives: a social history of middle-class Ireland 1882–1989*. Dublin. A&A Farmar.

Gilbert, J.T. 1854–59 *A history of the city of Dublin* (3 vols). Dublin. J. McGlashan & Co.

Gilligan, H.A. 1988 *A history of the port of Dublin*. Dublin. Gill & Macmillan.

Harvey, John 1949 *Dublin: a study in environment*. London, New York. Batsford.

Hickey, Kieran (ed.) 1973 *The light of other days: Irish life at the turn of the century in the photographs of Robert French*. London. Allen Lane.

Hickey, Kieran 1982 *Faithful departed: the Dublin of James Joyce's Ulysses*. Dublin. Ward River Press.

Horgan, Donald 2002 *The Victorian visitor in Ireland: Irish tourism 1840–1910*. Cork. Imagimedia.

Kearns, Kevin 1994 *Dublin tenement life: an oral history*. Dublin. Gill & Macmillan.

Kearns, Kevin 1998 *Dublin voices: an oral folk history*. Dublin. Gill & Macmillan.

Knowles, F.W.R. (n.d.) *Old Clontarf*. Dublin. The author.

Liddington, Jill and Crawford, Elizabeth 2011 '"Women do not count, neither shall they be counted": suffrage, citizenship and the battle for the 1911 census' in *History Workshop Journal* 7(1), 98–127.

Liddy, Pat 1987 *Dublin be proud: in celebration of Dublin's millennium year 1988*. Dublin. Chadworth.

Mac Thomáis, Éamonn 1977 *Me jewel and darlin' Dublin*. Dublin. O'Brien Press.

MacDonald, Frank 1985 *The destruction of Dublin*. Dublin. Gill & Macmillan.

McCarthy, Denis 1997 *Dublin Castle: at the heart of Irish history.* Dublin. Dublin Stationery Office.

McCullough, Niall 1989 *Dublin: an urban history.* Dublin. Anne Street Press.

McManus, Ruth 2002 *Dublin 1910–1940: shaping the city and suburbs.* Dublin. Four Courts Press.

Murphy, Cliona 1989 *The women's suffrage movement and Irish society in the early twentieth century.* Philadelphia. Temple University Press.

Nolan, William (ed.) 2005 *The Gaelic Athletic Association in Dublin 1884–2000.* Dublin. Geography Publications.

Peter, A. 1907 *Sketches of old Dublin.* Dublin. Sealy, Briars & Walker.

Prunty, Jacinta 1998 *Dublin slums, 1800–1925: a study in urban geography.* Dublin. Irish Academic Press.

Pritchett, V.S. 1967 *Dublin: a portrait.* London. Hogarth.

Pugh, Martin 2002 *The Pankhursts.* London. Penguin.

Purvis, June 2002 *Emmeline Pankhurst: a biography.* New York. Routledge.

Quinlan, Carmel 2002 *Genteel revolutionaries: Anna and Thomas Haslam and the Irish Women's Movement.* Cork. Cork University Press.

Ryan, Louise and Ward, Margaret (eds) 2007 *Irish women and the vote: becoming citizens.* Dublin. Irish Academic Press.

Simms, Anngret and Brady, Joseph (eds) 2001 *Dublin: through space and time.* Dublin. Four Courts Press.

Sisson, Elaine 2004 *Pearse's patriots: St Enda's and the cult of boyhood.* Cork. Cork University Press.

Ward, Margaret 1997 *Hanna Sheehy Skeffington: a life.* Dublin. Attic Press.

Wren, Jimmy 1987 *The villages of Dublin.* Dublin. Tomar.

ACKNOWLEDGEMENTS

The editor and the publisher are grateful to the following for their assistance and for permission to reproduce the items in this book: Chris Flynn and Niall O'Donnchú, Department of Arts, Heritage and the Gaeltacht; the National Library of Ireland, in particular Mary Broderick; Pauric Dempsey; Dr Paul Rouse, University College Dublin; Mark Duncan, Dr William Murphy for the use of his article on the suffragette movement; Independent News and Media, in particular Adrienne Carolan; The Irish Times Ltd; Stephen Ferguson, An Post Museum; Sergeant Paul Maher, the Garda Museum; Jessica O'Donnell, Dublin City Gallery The Hugh Lane; Nuala Canny, the National Botanic Gardens; Felix Larkin, the Kildare Street and University Club; Brian Crowley, the Pearse Museum; Máire Kennedy, Dublin City Library and Archive; the James Joyce Estate; Douglas Appleyard, Jacob Fruitfield Archive; Dr Gerald Mills and the Geography MA Class 2010–11, University College Dublin; Peter Lydon, Wesley College Archive; Eibhlín Roche, the Guinness Archive; the Institute for Astronomy, University of Vienna; the Irish Architectural Archive; the Irish Film Institute; Mary Lennon; the National Archives of Ireland; the National Gallery of Ireland; the Royal Irish Academy Library; Dónal Fenlon, the Royal Society of Antiquaries Ireland; the GAA Museum; the Scott Polar Research Centre, Cambridge University; Stephen Daglish; RTÉ Stills Archive; Tomás O'Riordan, University College Cork; the National Museums Northern Ireland, Ulster Folk and Transport Collection; the Museum of London; the University of Cornell; Adam's Fine Art Auctioneers and Valuers; Alex Ward, the National Museum of Ireland; Sue Holt, Mike Holt British Stamps; Dr Robin Govier, *Irish Naturalists' Journal*; Professor Tom Ray, MRIA; Dr Elaine Sisson, Dun Laoghaire Institute of Art, Design and Technology; Dr Luca Crispi, University College Dublin; Professor Anne Fogarty, University College Dublin; Gjenvick-Gjønvik Archives; CardCow Vintage Postcards; the Advertising Archives; Corbis Images; Getty Images.

The essays owe an enormous debt to the many authors who have written about life in Dublin over the years. The work of Professor Mary E. Daly, MRIA; Dr Jacinta Prunty; Dr Ruth McManus; Dr Christine Casey; Dr Douglas Bennett and Dr Kevin Kearns, in particular, laid the foundations on which this book is built and their influence on the text is evident throughout. This book could not have been written without their work and their contribution to the historiography of Dublin has been immense.

Old Cromac

Old Cromac Whisky is made in the Cromac Distillery from the finest IRISH barley. Every bottle is guaranteed by the distillers to be not less than 12 years old, and the exact particulars of age are printed plainly on every label.

Ask for **Old Cromac**

—the Whisky with the guaranteed age.

Look for the guarantee